DATE			

The Alaska Gold Rush

RANDOM HOUSE · NEW YORK

THE
ALASKA
GOLD RUSH

by
May McNeer

Illustrated by LYND WARD

contents

Come one! come all!

It was the summer of 1897. For four years people all over the United States had been worried. Times were bad. So many had no jobs. So many had too little to eat. So many couldn't pay their rent, or keep up the interest payments on mortgages. Those who could, took the small funds that they had left and turned them into gold pieces. These they hid in holes, in closets, under mattresses, in old socks. They said, "I have to have a nest egg. If things get worse I'll have my hoard of gold." They were in a panic of fear—fear of starvation.

There was too much gold hidden away in small piles of coins. There just wasn't enough money being spent for anything. Those who made goods and those who raised food saw their sales dwindle. Those who handled these things—railroad men, truckers, storekeepers—were sitting around with little to do.

One morning newspapers everywhere came out with a story that made readers' eyes pop. GOLD! GOLD STRIKE IN THE KLONDIKE!

In Chicago a man calmly eating breakfast and wondering how long he was going to keep his job pulled his newspaper closer to his face. "Alaska? The Klondike? How far away is Alaska? Where is this Klondike?" He read aloud to his wife, and kept on reading.

"This paper says they've found gold up there. It says that Alaska is big—twice as big as Texas. It's shaped like a frying pan, with the handle along the coast of the Pacific Ocean, and the pan sticking out towards Siberia, on the Bering Sea.

"Alaska is a funny word. Says here it's an Aleut word, meaning 'Great Country.' It sounds great! It's full of mountains, and one is the tallest on the continent—Mount McKinley, over twenty thousand feet high.

"It says that Klondike comes from the Indian word *Thron-diuck*, meaning 'the place where fish nets are hung on stakes.' That's a name for you, isn't it? The Klondike is a river, and it's in Canadian Northwest Territory. Gold is in just one spot—the Valley of the Klondike River.

"The gold's in Canada, I guess. And you have to get there through Alaska. But when you get

there, there's a lot of it. It's just lying around on the ground in nuggets as big as duck eggs."

He leaped from his chair and ran to his bed. Then he pulled a lumpy sock from under his mattress, and emptied its contents on the table. "Gold! This ought to be enough to buy a pan, a pick, a shovel, and enough grub to last me until I make a fortune for us."

Down in Alabama a young man was reading a newspaper too. His two hound dogs were stretched out at his feet. He read aloud, slowly.

"What kind of a place is this Alaska? Says here it's an American Territory up there on the Arctic Circle. To get there by land you have to cross Canada, or go by ship. Says it's got a lot of Indian tribes, but the place is so big there are hardly any people to see up there. It says there are a few towns, though, on the panhandle. Like Sitka, the capital, and Juneau, where they've been taking out a little gold from hard rock for nearly twenty years. But the new gold strike is five hundred miles north of Juneau. It's on a branch of the Yukon, called the Klondike.

"Says they've been mining some all around towns on the Yukon called Fortymile and Circle. But they've never seen anything like the gold on the Klondike. I wonder now—I wonder——"

His mother, rocking back and forth near by, nodded her head. "I've heard about Alaska. Your father knew a man who went to Juneau once, and came back to tell about it. It's the largest country you ever heard of—and the coldest. Everything's big up there. He said they have the biggest bears in the world—Kodiaks, and grizzlies—and polar bears up on the Arctic where the Eskimos are. He said they have the hottest summers, too, as hot as here, and the coldest winters—seventy below, maybe. They have the biggest flowers, too—daisies look like sunflowers. Anyway, that's what he said."

The young man read aloud again, with a look on his face as if he were under some kind of spell. "This paper says that Alaska was bought by the United States from the Russians in 1867. The Russians were getting furs and fish there. Up in the Klondike Valley the gold's just lying around on top of the ground, like peaches in the orchard yonder. I'm going! I've made up my mind. That money I've been saving to buy bottom land will pay my way."

He jumped up, and the dogs followed him indoors. His mother called after him, "What'll the hounds do without you, son?"

"I'll take 'em along. That paper said sleds are pulled by dogs. There aren't any better hound dogs than mine. They'll pull me over the snow."

In Tombstone, Arizona, a widow who kept a boarding house heard some talk of gold in the

Klondike. "What's that Klondike, anyway?" she wondered. Around town everybody was talking about Alaska and the Klondike. One after another men were getting ready to go. The widow decided to go too. She was sure that many things would be needed in the Klondike. All those men keeping house for themselves! Their cabins must be filthy. She would take a big load of brooms with her and sell them for an enormous price. Why, she would make a fortune! She brought out her savings, and made plans to give up her boarding house and start out for Alaska and the Klondike.

A man and his wife bent over a newspaper spread on their table in Toronto, Canada, and talked of the Klondike. A brother, just arrived from New York, unrolled the newspaper he had brought with him. Both papers were filled with the same excitement.

"All that gold! They scoop it up by the ton."

"I'm on my way."

"I'll go with you," said the Toronto man.

"I'll go too," said his wife. "And we'll take my new piano, of course."

"Now, how can we do that? A piano!"

"We'll just take it apart, pack the works in cotton batting, and carry it all along in pieces. We will buy a wagon." She leaned over the newspaper again. "Now which way do we go? We can take a ship from Vancouver to White Pass, or to Chilkoot Pass, in Alaska, and then go by trail over the mountains. But that looks hard. Or we can take a ship up to the mouth of the Yukon and then a river boat all the way to the gold fields. But that's three thousand miles from Vancouver. It would take too long. We can go with horse and a wagon from Edmonton, on the Canadian prairie. We'd go by land all the way, and not have to cross the United States or Alaska at all. That's the best way."

The Klondike was a magic word. So was Alaska. In Germany, Sweden, England, Africa, Brazil—everywhere the words crackled like electricity. "Klondike? I'm off tomorrow." "Alaska? Where do I get my ticket?" Gold. Klondike. Klondike gold! The rainbow in front of everybody's eyes arched over the frozen North. And the pot of gold was in Alaska and the Klondike.

That's where the gold was, all right. But who found it? How did all this get started?

2

Siwash george

In the spring of 1896 talk of gold was not new in the vast northern land where the two-thousand-mile-long Yukon River wound its way through both Canadian and American territories. The Russians, who had come first, after the Eskimos and Indians, had built several trading-post towns. One of them was St. Michaels, sixty-five miles north of the mouth of the Yukon River. The Russians had not come for gold. Only furs and fish were valuable to them. When a trapper came in with a handful of nuggets the Russian governor shouted, "Never bring gold here! We want only furs and fish. Gold will bring Americans. They will ruin our trade."

Yet Americans did come in, in small numbers, a few at a time. They all went hunting for gold.

They wandered up to the Arctic Circle, where Eskimo tribes hunt seal and walrus. They went into the panhandle to the south, along the coast, where the Haidas and the Tlingit Indians had their tall, carved totem poles and wooden houses. They even tried to go east, toward the great Mackenzie River, but were forced back by fierce Crooked Eye Indians, and other savage tribes.

By 1896 prospectors had been wandering up the Yukon, into the valleys of its tributaries, and along little creeks, for fifteen years. They were the sourdoughs. The sourdough was a miner who had spent at least one winter in this lonely place. He had seen the river ice break with a roar and a crash in spring. He was the miner who had been there long enough to keep a can of yeasty dough hanging above the stove in his cabin. Each day he would pinch off a little and use it to make his new batch of bread rise.

A sourdough always looked with some scorn at a *cheechaco*, or tenderfoot. They were all called prospectors while they hunted for a good claim to stake. They were miners when they began to work the claim, after it had been put on record legally.

These sourdoughs had a gambling spirit, and they were foot-loose men, always on the search for "luck." Most of them had come north from the California Gold Rush of 1849, when the loose gold in the streams and hillsides there had all been taken out. What did it matter if they were

9

cold, dirty, lonely, or often hungry? The cry of "Gold strike!" sent them running to a new location.

George Carmack was one of those prospectors who had been grubstaked by a storekeeper, promising to pay up his bill for food when he came in with a strike. Unlike most of the others, he was not exclusively a prospector. He had other connections too. He was known as Siwash George because he had an Indian wife, and he was often out with his wife's relatives catching and drying salmon. George Carmack liked Indians, and he resented the way some men looked down on them. But he spent part of his time hunting for gold. Sourdoughs thought him a mighty good liar, and laughed at his stories. They laughed loudest of all when he came in over the snows to Fortymile and told them of a dream he had just had. Winking, nudging each other, they grinned, and listened.

Siwash George told them that the night before he had dreamed he was on a creek in the Klondike Valley. He was standing beside the stream, watching the fish called graylings leap in the sun as they struggled up the rapids on the way to their spawning grounds. Suddenly he saw two enormous, golden salmon jump high in the air and bound over the white water. They landed right in front of him. He couldn't believe his sight, for instead of fish scales they had golden nuggets all over them. As they lay there looking

at him he realized that each king salmon had golden coins for eyes.

When Siwash George stopped talking everybody roared with laughter. As he shrugged, and went out to return to the Indian tribe, they shouted after him. "Say, Siwash, that's the best lie yet. Come back and tell us another!"

When the mighty river had broken into flood and summer had come, George, with his wife Kate, and their daughter Graphie Gracey, were putting their salmon catch over racks to dry in the sun. With them they had two Indian friends, little Tagish Charley and a giant called Skookum Jim, which means "big and strong." George heard a hail from up the creek bank, and saw a white man of his acquaintance standing there.

Robert Henderson was a quiet, unsmiling Scotsman, and a real sourdough. He believed in the code of the miners—never to keep news of a good gold strike to one's self.

"Some boys and I have panned out a fairly good prospect up on the Klondike," he called out. "About eight cents' worth of gold to the pan. I'm on my way out for supplies now. There's room for you to stake, George. But no Indians. We don't want Indians there."

Siwash George nodded, and talked to him awhile. After Henderson left George took his wife and daughter, Tagish Charley, and Skookum Jim along with him. They headed in the general direction of the Klondike River. On a little creek called the Rabbit, Carmack's wife picked up some gravel and showed it to George. Jim and Charley bent over it too. George was not impressed.

"A little color in there," he admitted. "We'd probably make more money cutting logs and rafting them to Fortymile. But it *is* gold. There's a bit of color in that gravel."

Skookum Jim and Tagish Charley were more anxious to prospect than Carmack was, but he decided to try it too. Fighting off the swarms of mosquitoes, they made camp among the wild flowers along the creek. While George slept under a tree Skookum Jim took the frying pan to the creek and began to wash out some gravel. George jumped to his feet at a shout from Jim. "Gold!" George went to look, and his eyes grew excited. That pan held gold worth at least three dollars. A big strike! No other strike he had ever heard of had brought in that much to a pan. The usual worth of a good strike was about twenty cents of gold to a pan. Skookum Jim and Tagish Charley staked out their claims on that creek. Siwash George drove in his stakes also. Logs and the good price for lumber were forgotten. Carmack was filled with excitement. But, remembering the remarks about Indians, he decided not to go and tell Henderson, as he was expected to do. He cut a deep blaze on a tree with his axe. On the streak of white wood he wrote in pencil:

"To whom it may concern. I do, this day,

locate and claim, by right of discovery, five hundred running feet, running up stream from this notice. Located this 17th day of August, 1896."

Carmack left Skookum Jim to guard the claims and, with Tagish Charley, went out to make the official records in Fortymile. Canadian mining laws were strict, and were enforced by the Mounted Police. One claim to a miner, they said, and the claim must be recorded according to law.

On the way Carmack and Tagish Charley overtook two half-starving French Canadians trying to reach Fortymile before their beans and bacon gave out. These men had prospected without success in the Yukon region for years, and were

at the point where they wondered whether McQuesten would grubstake them again.

"We've made a strike on Rabbit Creek," Carmack told them. "Better get up there, boys!"

The men looked at each other and laughed. They didn't believe Siwash George. Nobody did. Then George took out his cartridge case and opened it. The case was filled with golden nuggets. The bearded, ragged French Canadians stared, speechless. Then they yelled, threw up their hats, and ran for their canoe. Grabbing duffle and the little food that they had left, they took off into the hills like fleeing moose. Carmack and Tagish Charley laughed and moved on.

After a while they met more men drifting around, looking for something worth staking out and not really expecting to find it. Two Scotsmen had heard of the strike made by Henderson, and stopped to ask about it. Siwash George told them about his find and at the first sight of the cartridge case they took off also. Carmack mentioned his find to everybody he met along the river on the way to Fortymile. He was willing to tell everybody but Henderson.

In the little miners' town where shacks leaned together about the Alaska Commercial Company's trading store, Siwash George strolled slowly into the saloon and called out, "We've struck pay dirt on Rabbit Creek!"

Some of the bystanders snorted and turned away. A few laughed and said, "Another bluff.

15

What are you trying to do, start a stampede?"

Again Carmack slowly opened his cartridge case, and the contents rolled out on the counter. Men leaped forward, eyes popping. These were old sourdoughs who had been in the Yukon country for years. They could recognize the gold from different areas. They saw that these nuggets were different, richer than any they had ever seen. As Carmack and Tagish Charley moved along to the police post to record their claims, the little town of Fortymile emptied suddenly. Every miner there made a rush for his grub, his pick, pan, shovel, and tent. Every skin canoe and rickety wooden boat and, in fact, anything that would float or could be paddled, rowed, or poled, filled instantly and was pushed off upstream. The air was raucous with shouts and excited yells:

"Whoopee! Get going, boys. Strike on Rabbit Creek!"

Some who went really believed it, because they had seen Carmack's gold. Others went without believing, because they were sourdoughs and they had to be in on any excitement.

3

The golden pup

A big strike on the Klondike! The sourdoughs were coming. There weren't more than a few hundred of them in all of northern Alaska and the Canadian Northwest Territory. Yet, somehow, the word traveled fast, and they came up the Yukon in Indian skin canoes, on rafts, in scows. They also came on foot. The Klondike River flows into the Yukon, from east to west, through flat-topped hills. It joins the mighty river about five hundred miles north of the Pacific Ocean, and just around five hundred miles south of the Arctic Ocean. It is not so far from the boundary of Alaska.

In a few days prospectors were digging and staking claims on Rabbit Creek, which was immediately re-named. It became Bonanza Creek.

Bonanza means "rich with wealth or gold." In a few weeks there were so many frantic prospectors staking claims that for several miles up and down the creek from Carmack's strike Bonanza was all taken.

Not all of the first comers found much gold on their new claims. It was a matter of luck. Clarence Berry was one of the unlucky ones. He had come to the north from California, pulling his wife behind him on a sled. But his claim on Bonanza yielded so little gold that he grew discouraged.

He left his wife in the mining town of Forty-mile and, taking his pick and shovel and pan, went to the diggings. From time to time he stopped work and went to watch others to see what they were getting. This was a kind of mining called "placer." It was done by scooping gravel from the creek bed into a round, flat pan with sides like a big pie-pan. Then the prospector would squat on his heels on the edge of the stream, fill the pan with water, and move it around and around, letting the dirt and water slosh out over the side. The gold, being heavy, would remain in the bottom of the pan.

Washing out gold in a pan—or "panning it"—isn't hard. But soon there wasn't much more gravel to wash out of the stream beds where the strike had been made. Then digging must begin. Berry watched miners picking out a spot and then doing what was called "Yukon digging." This was not like digging in any other gold field, for here the ground under a layer of mud was always frozen. To thaw it men had to build fires on it so that they could dig. When they had taken some dirt out, they put it into a rocker. This was shaped like a cradle. As one man dumped in dirt or gravel, his partner poured in water and then rocked it like a cradle. The water took away the dirt, leaving gold in the cleats, or riffles, that were nailed into it on a sloping board.

Some miners built long sluice boxes also, called long-Toms. These carried water and dirt downhill, leaving gold in the riffles, as in a rocker. Sometimes pans of black sand were taken out, and the gold was settled in the bottom with the use of mercury.

When Berry grew discouraged he went back to Fortymile and took a job as assistant bartender. To the saloon one night came another discouraged miner, who told Clarence Berry his story. He was Antone Stander, a handsome young Austrian, who had been among the early comers to Bonanza Creek. Stander had watched Siwash George Carmack sweating under a load of gravel which he had to carry on his back to the creek for washing. Carmack had no money yet—not enough to buy a wheelbarrow, or tools to build a sluice box.

Stander was too late to get a claim on Bonanza, and he and his four partners were wandering about, just looking. After a while he walked through the underbrush over a tiny stream that ran through a little gulch and then into Bonanza. This stream was too small to have a name and was referred to by the miners as "Bonanza's pup."

Other prospectors did not think "the pup" large enough to consider for claims. The tiny stream at the bottom of the gulch was so small that it could scarcely be seen through the thick bushes and trees. Stander's partners followed him, and saw him stoop down at the creek to wash out a pan of gravel.

"What are you doing that for?" called out one of them with some irritation. "You're just wasting time. This couldn't be a place to find any 'color'."

Stander slowly stood up. His eyes gleamed. He held out his pan and his partners leaned over for a look. They saw color—the rich color of gold. They saw so much that it made them gasp. This pan held at least five or six dollars' worth of gold! They stared at each other, speechless, and then they talked in excited whispers. No longer were sourdoughs spreading the news of a new strike. Now it was each man for himself.

They went back to Fortymile to record their claims, and they named "the pup" Eldorado. (Eldorado was the name of the fabulously rich legendary city of gold, in South America, built on a lake where gold was thrown in as a sacrifice to a god called the Golden Man.)

Stander went to Fortymile trying to think of a way to get a grubstake, or supplies and tools enough to work his claim. He had a good claim, but he had to have credit. McQuesten would have given him credit, but McQuesten was in Circle City, more than two hundred miles downriver. In Fortymile the store was owned by the Alaska Commercial Company, and run by Edgar Mizner.

Mizner had come here with his brothers— Addison, an architect, and Wilson, a spendthrift who was always the most popular man in any group that he joined. But Edgar wasn't. The things that the miners said about Edgar warmed the air even on a cold day. The Mizners were sons of a San Francisco family, formerly wealthy, but now unable to live in the style that they were used to. The boys were out for adventure, and here they were finding it.

Stander asked Edgar Mizner for credit to work his claim.

"Who do you think you are?" demanded Mizner. "I don't give credit to anybody unless he has backing. If you want to be grubstaked find a man who will stand good if you fail to pay up."

So Stander went into McPhee's saloon and told his troubles to Clarence Berry, the assistant bartender.

Berry nodded. "Sounds good, Stander. Think Mizner would let me back you? I have a steady job."

"Don't know. Let's go see."

They came away from the store loaded with provisions and tools. Stander and Berry made a deal on their claims. They traded half of Berry's claims on Bonanza for half of Stander's claim on Eldorado.

Then the news got out. There was a rush to Eldorado—men scrambling and clawing about among the bushes to drive in stakes, and running back to town to record them as fast as they could get there.

Clarence Berry went out to his claim, and made a rich strike. He built a tiny windowless cabin of logs, and his wife joined him. While he worked the claim she kept house, her furniture consisting of a homemade table, bunks, and boxes for seats. She had her stove, of course, with the sourdough can dangling above it. When Clarence had time, and could find one, he shot a moose. Otherwise they lived on beans, bacon and bread. Ethel Berry did have fish, when she could walk far enough away to find any. The fish of these streams were all caught, or driven far away. Yet, whenever she felt like it, Mrs. Berry could go out and pick up a handful of gold from the dump of earth beside her husband's new mine.

This tiny creek called Eldorado was the richest stream of its size in the whole world! All who had claims on it were becoming millionaires. Along all of the streams running into the Klondike, miners were swapping claims, or selling, or buying "lays." A "lay" was a rental of a claim for a certain sum, for a certain length of time. The man who rented the claim—or the "lay"—could have all of the gold that he found. This was a gamble and it caused considerable excitement. Sometimes a miner who thought his claim was worthless would try to unload it on a dupe if he couldn't find somebody to take a "lay" on it.

Charley Anderson was thought to be a dupe. He was a Swede who bought a claim for eight hundred dollars, and heard the sourdoughs laughing at him. They said that he "sure was a sucker. That claim is no good." Anderson asked the Mounted Police in Fortymile to get his money back, but was told that the deal was legal. So Charley squared his shoulders and trudged off to work his claim anyway. Everybody repeated the joke about the big Swede. Then they stopped laughing. For his claim produced a million dollars in gold for him. And instead of being called a "sucker" Charley Anderson became known as the "lucky Swede."

Gold was stored up in cabins along Bonanza and Eldorado. It was kept in old tin cans, pickle bottles, socks, or pokes of moosehide or sealskin. It was even wrapped in newspapers tied with strings.

In the digging there was only one woman other than Mrs. Clarence Berry. She was Mrs. Tom Lippy, wife of a former Y.M.C.A. teacher. The two women didn't see much of each other. But Mrs. Lippy also lived in a log cabin, with nothing to cook but flour, bacon and beans. She could also bring in a handful of gold whenever she wanted to go to the dump beside her husband's hole in the frozen ground.

Laws on claims were strictly enforced by the Mounties. When a claim was abandoned it was open for another staking after a period of sixty days. On Bonanza some claims were nearing the end of the waiting period and could then be put on record under a new name. One in particular was thought to be a rich one. Although it was November, with heavy snow on the ground and

the temperature dropping below zero, two men—
a Scotsman and a Swede—made up their minds
to get that claim. It was to be a race for it.
"And the best man wins!"

Miners gathered and built bonfires on the
snow. At midnight the two men, a Scotsman and
a Swede, pounded in their stakes on the same
ground. Then they jumped for their dog sleds,
and their teams raced for Fortymile.

Faster! Faster! The dogs streaked down the
frozen river, and were soon out of sight of the
shouting, cheering miners. It was as dark as the
inside of a mine. Then the northern lights sent
bands of green, red, blue and white arching and
streaming across the black sky. Faster! Faster!
The dogs panted and strained. The drivers
gasped with the cold and pushed forward with

their feet, as if trying to run with the huskies.

The winner had to reach the office before four in the afternoon. In Fortymile it was nearly four. Overhead the lights had faded and disappeared with morning, and dusk of early afternoon was changing to night. The whole town was out watching for the racing dog teams. Then they came. The Scotsman leaped out of his sled and ran. The Swede jumped down and made a dash for it. They beat their dog teams to the town. The Swede made for a big building that looked like an office to him. Then he saw his rival heading for another building, and he wheeled toward that. As the Scotsman fell over the open doorway, shouting, "Sixty above on Bonanza!" the Swede came in on top of him.

The recorder asked the Mounted Police officer, Inspector Constantine, to decide this contest. Constantine told the two men to divide it. This they did—and when they went to work on the claim they found it to be worthless.

It was a good race, though. "The fastest dog race ever I see in my life," said a miner, shifting his tobacco plug to the other cheek. "And I've seen a-plenty of dog races in my time up here—from Eskimos to Indians. But these boys outdistanced the malamutes. I never did see human beings run as fast as that Scotchman and that Swede."

4

The magic town

One man who came in with the early prospectors became a storekeeper, selling food and tools to the miners. His name was LeRoy Napoleon McQuesten. McQuesten was a big fellow who had wanted to be a voyageur for the Hudson's Bay Company. Yet, when he tried to compete with the French Canadians, some of them smaller than he, he could not do it. He could not carry as heavy a pack or stand the long hours paddling the big bateaux, as the canoes were called. So for fifteen years McQuesten prospected for gold all over the territory. He found very little. Then he settled down with an Indian wife and built trading posts at Circle City, in Alaska, and at Fortymile, in Canada—both on the Yukon River.

By the year 1896 there was a chain of small settlements on the Yukon, separated from one another by considerable distances. These included Fort Yukon, Fortymile, Sixtymile, Fort Reliance, and the Indian town of Moosehide. McQuesten owned a small steamboat, the *New Racket,* one of the only two on the Yukon. All miners and prospectors liked that Scotsman, McQuesten. He grubstaked them. In other words, he let them have food and other supplies for prospecting or mining all winter without paying for them. Then he collected, if he could, when they brought in enough gold in the spring.

In Circle City storekeeper McQuesten ran the whole town. The settlement had sprung up in 1894 when gold had been discovered in several creeks draining into the Yukon near Circle. At the time when Siwash George brought news of his strike to Fortymile, claims around Circle were bringing in twenty cents to the pan. Circle City miners had brought into town a million dollars in gold dust. Circle had a school, a little library, and even a theater where the plays of William Shakespeare were sometimes performed.

In January, 1896, miners began to gather in small groups, talking excitedly.

"Hear about the Klondike? They say Carmack's found more gold there than anybody ever saw before."

"Carmack? Old lying Siwash George? You can't believe him. I'm going to stay with my claim right here on Preacher's Creek."

In a miner's cabin on Porcupine Creek not far from Circle City an old sourdough offered coffee to two passing prospectors. They came into his cabin, warmed by its sheet-tin Yukon stove with the inevitable can of yeasty dough swinging overhead. As they stamped the snow from their boots and sat down on the bunk, they both talked at once.

They were in a hurry, and drank scalding coffee as fast as they could, eating mouthfuls of beans and bread as they talked.

"Biggest strike you ever heard of. Richer pans than anybody ever saw around here. On the Klondike. Where? Don't know exactly, but somewhere up the Yukon beyond Fortymile. Why, we heard they are getting four dollars to the pan—sometimes five or six!"

The old men were scornful. "Don't believe it. Big talk like that can't stir me. I heard that Siwash George brought in some yarn to Fortymile. But a man's a fool to rush off somewhere because of a piece of wild talk. I've got a good claim here."

The two visitors put on snowshoes and pushed off. The old sourdough stood looking around his little log cabin. He had worked hard here. He had chinked the cracks in the logs with moss, to keep out Arctic winds. He had sodded the roof with clumps of earth and moss, and in summer he had wild grasses growing up there. He had been here two years.

Suddenly he began to move, running around as if the cabin had caught fire. With a wild gleam in his eyes he dashed about gathering up his frying pan and coffee pot, still hot from breakfast. He folded his extra clothing into a pack, and then tied his axe, shovel and pick to it. He stuffed his cooking utensils into his pack too. Then he stamped out into the snow to his storehouse, which was built on poles behind the house. He brought in his few cans of food, and shoved them into the pack. Then he threw on his mackinaw coat, pulled on his boots, and pushed the door wide open. He hauled his sled out. When he had tied his gear on he pulled the sled behind him and followed in the snow-shoe tracks left by his visitors.

It was dark all winter, day and night, in the Arctic. But the old sourdough was used to that. Behind him his snug cabin stood open to the whirling snow. The door, blown by the wind, swung back and forth on its leather hinges. Already the cabin looked forlorn and empty. It would soon sink down into a heap of logs.

All Circle City was pushing off upriver. In the deadly cold, with a temperature of sixty below zero, men hitched up their dog teams. With a terrific snapping and howling, the malamutes and huskies bounded off on the solidly frozen river.

Those who had no dogs, like the old sourdough from Porcupine Creek, pulled their own sleds.

Some walked, with packs on their backs, hoping to make better time and get the best claims.

Big McQuesten watched his town leave, and worried as he stood at his store window. He knew the miners. They always jumped into action with the speed of a firehorse at the smell of smoke. Circle City had a population of more than a thousand, not counting the wandering miners who came and went. Now the entire town, every living person, seemed to be leaving. And the dogs were going too. McQuesten told himself that this was all a hoax. The boys would come struggling back to their claims in a few weeks, or months, at the most.

One of the men who left in a hurry was Joseph Ladue. But he wasn't interested in staking a claim in the new gold diggings. He had other ideas, and they were to make him richer than most of the sourdoughs slogging through the snows. Ladue knew the country up there on the Yukon, and he knew the Klondike. There were no towns close enough to the new strike. He would start one.

When Ladue reached the place where the Klondike poured into the Yukon, he saw a flat, marshy stretch of ground along the two streams. Behind it rose a high hill. Here Ladue filed his claim to land—acres of it. He brought in the machinery for a sawmill, put men to work cutting logs, and built a big warehouse. He sold both lumber and town lots.

A few miners pitched their tents around the warehouse. Some enterprising fellows bought lots from Ladue, and started to build a few stores. Tents were replaced by shacks and log cabins. Overnight, as if by magic, there was a town called Dawson City. Soon miners were coming in and going out, paying for their supplies with gold dust and nuggets from their rawhide bags. (They called these their pokes.) Soon plank sidewalks echoed in the dusky daylight with the sound of hobnailed boots. The air was filled with the sound of huskies howling and men shouting, and always the noise of sawing and hammering. Soon there were Indian packers, wagons, and a few horses. Dawson City was pungent with the scent of sawdust, garbage, whiskey, animals, men, and wood smoke from hundreds of Yukon stoves. The Mounted Police sent in a squad of men to keep order.

There was plenty of gold, but very little to buy with it. There was no hay. The few horses in Dawson had to be fed on bread and bacon, and so they learned to eat man's food. The wife of one of the Mounties had two hens, and she sold eggs for a dollar each. There was so much gold that few looked at it as it was poured out on counters. But the sight of a loaf of fresh bread baked by Mrs. Wills, who came up from Circle to open a tent bakery, drew a crowd. This woman sold a loaf of bread for a dollar, and also started a small laundry. When she got those going well, she went out prospecting, found a good claim and worked it herself. In the end she took a quarter of a million dollars out of that claim. The bakery and the laundry were money-makers, too.

The cold was so intense that men had to keep their heads covered while they slept. If they didn't they would wake to find their faces frozen. They were hungry most of the time, but they staked their claims, and they continued to dig. The sourdoughs built fires on the snow and kept them going day and night, in order to thaw the earth beneath. And then they dug out the dirt and threw it on their frozen dump, piling it up until they could wash it out in the summer.

Back in Circle City McQuesten realized at last that the boys weren't coming back. Circle City was a ghost town now, with all of the doors swinging open in the wind and snow. He packed his gear and went to the Klondike too, to stake out a claim for himself and start working it.

5

Treasure ships

In the summer of 1897, nearly a year after Siwash George Carmack had found his rich claim in the Klondike Valley, two ships loaded with gold arrived in two Pacific Coast ports. One of them, the *Portland*, docked in Seattle, Washington. The other, the *Excelsior*, steamed in through the Golden Gate and nosed in beside a wharf at San Francisco.

In their city of hills, San Franciscans climbed the steep streets as if nothing especially exciting was happening. One woman stopped to tell a friend that Willie was out of work again, and to remark that jobs were as scarce as hens' teeth. And prices! Outrageous. Steak was fifteen cents a pound. You had to pay a dollar and a half a week for an apartment. How could poor people live with such prices? And gold was so scarce that it was worth twice as much as its value in paper money.

The gangplank of the squat little ship, the *Excelsior*, came down with a rattle and a bang. Some men waiting around the wharf for work moved closer.

"Where's she from? St. Michael's in Alaska? Up on the Bering Sea? You don't say!"

Down the gangplank staggered a curious procession of passengers bent under heavy loads. They were bearded miners wearing rough clothing made for cold weather. Their faces had been burned almost black by the blazing arctic sun and the fierce cold wind. The bags and valises they carried were so heavy that some of them had to be hauled by two or three men. Their eyes under their winter caps were gleaming.

"Gold in those sacks? Really? Gold. Gold dust from Alaska. Gold nuggets from the Klondike. What's the Klondike?"

"Don't know what it is or where it is. But there's tons of gold on board that ship. Look! Just look at that!"

Down the gangplank came two miners dragging a heavy blanket tied securely by its corners. They hailed a wagon.

"That couldn't be full of gold. By George, it must be!"

The crowd grew as if by magic. Reporters from the San Francisco *Call* and other newspapers pushed into the milling jam. Thomas Lippy, the former Y.M.C.A. man, came ashore with his sunburned wife, Salome, dressed in the baggy heavy clothing of the frozen wilds. They were on the way to becoming millionaires. Together they carried a suitcase so heavy with gold that they could hardly lift it, even though Tom Lippy was a big and muscular fellow. Joe Ladue followed, bringing in the huge lot of gold he had taken in as pay for lots and lumber and other commodities in the bulging town of Dawson.

Then the whole of San Francisco seemed to pour down toward the dirty little two-stack steamship. The last miners off were almost knocked over by frantic men and women eager to hear how they had found all this wealth. But the miners managed to hire wagons and cabs. Because the United States Mint was closed they took their gold directly to a smelting works. There it was poured out on a counter to be weighed and paid for.

Telegraph wires hummed with the news. Newspapers all over the world carried the same headlines: GOLD ON THE KLONDIKE! GOLD IN ALASKA! SHIPS COMING IN LADEN WITH GOLD. Until July 15th, 1897, who had ever heard of that Northern Indian word—Klondike? Now, who in the world hadn't?

The two little Pacific Ocean steamships, the *Excelsior* and the *Portland*, had both been in port in St. Michaels in June when the first small boats came down the Yukon from Dawson with their loads of miners and gold. They had started out from Alaska at about the same time. But the *Portland* was a slower boat, and she reached Seattle two days after the *Excelsior* had docked in San Francisco. The *Portland* too was crammed with rich miners, including Mr. and Mrs. Clarence

Berry and stylish Mrs. Gage, daughter-in-law of the United States Secretary of the Treasury. Mrs. Gage wore a somewhat shabby but fashionable gown with velvet trimmings on the long skirt and huge leg-of-mutton sleeves. Ethel Berry had on the woolen outfit of a male prospector. Yet the Berrys were now worth almost a million dollars.

The *Portland* was no surprise to Seattle. Word of the treasure-laden *Excelsior* and her sister ship had come by crackling telegraph wire from San Francisco. She was escorted through the harbor by a tug filled with newspaper reporters. At the dock she was greeted by almost the whole population of the city.

Seattle became a madhouse. Doctors, clerks, butchers, lawyers, and barbers dropped their work. They rushed into stores for outfits. Every horse, mule and dog in sight was bought and made ready to go. Nobody could ride the street cars because motormen and conductors had left them standing idle while they rushed off to buy supplies to take to Alaska and the Klondike.

San Francisco was in the same frenzy. A wife calmly frying pork chops heard her husband dash into the house and grab their carefully hoarded gold pieces from under the mattress. He ran to the stores to buy picks, pans, shovels, and a mackinaw coat, and booked passage on a ship for the north. Every boat, tub or ship of any possible use was put into service to Alaska.

Summer fruit rotted on the ground because

pickers were going to the gold fields. In Chicago, New York, Philadelphia—in almost every city, town and hamlet in the country—men scurried about for supplies and gear. Stores boomed, money was again in circulation, and nobody thought of hard times now.

Gold! That magic word. It meant far more to everybody than the gleaming metal could possibly be worth just by itself. It meant a dream, excitement—adventure! It brought out the gambling instinct in people who didn't know they had it.

Women caught it too. Some outfitted themselves like the men, and were on their way west. Others prepared to accompany their husbands. Nobody stopped to realize that this was a vast unknown land, cruel and bleak to strangers. Nor did it occur to them how long a trip inland lay ahead if and when they reached Alaska; or that after early August it would be impossible to get to the diggings before freeze-up. Indeed, they didn't know what freeze-up really meant in the land of the midnight sun.

They opened newspapers that carried sensational stories: "Fabulous fortunes picked up in the loose dirt along the streams of Alaska!" They read magazines telling them that gold lay around in nuggets as big as hens' eggs. The stories did not mention the fact that most of the ground was frozen solid even in summer, and that mining by hand in that country was brutal, hard labor. They did not mention that a real hen's egg cost a dollar, and that it was quite possible to starve with a poke full of gold in hand when there was no way to buy food.

Around the world swept the news. "Gold in the North! Get there fast! Easy to reach, over the mountains or by river. Buy your outfits here. Get your boat tickets there." Bank presidents bought outfits and tickets on ships that were leaky crates. So did gamblers.

Out in Colorado, a man named Jefferson Randolph Smith who was originally from the South decided to go to Alaska. He had visions of salting away a fortune, but no intention of digging for it. He was more often called "Soapy" than Jeff. This was in honor of his skill in palming off on the innocent public cakes of soap which he persuaded them to believe had twenty-dollar bills in the wrappers. Soapy was a bunko man known to the sheriffs and marshalls in Creede, in Denver, and elsewhere in the West. He was going to "take over" the little tent camp called Skagway.

Ships from Australia, South America, Europe, all headed for the northern land of Bonanza and Eldorado. They were loaded to the rails with excited men. Horses, dogs, cattle and sheep were crammed into the holds of vessels that looked as if they would sink before morning.

During those first months the news burst like a flaming rocket, firing the imaginations of men and women everywhere. People dreamed of golden nuggets. They were in a mood to believe anything. They paid any price, however high, for a ticket to the west coast, or a fare on a ship. Entertainers, gamblers, thieves and card sharps embarked as fast as they could get passage.

The talk was wild. Somebody had a grand project to start a balloon transport for miners. Another promoted the "Klondike bicycle" for riding all the way overland. Otherwise sensible, respectable men and women seemed to catch the fever overnight. Every eccentric in the land appeared determined to be in on the Gold Rush. And many of them were.

All through that autumn and winter, ship after ship took excited and ignorant cheechacos and dumped them on the rocky shores of Alaska, or took them up the marshes of the lower Yukon. They came by the hundreds, by the thousands.

The crazy stampede was thundering madly across the face of the continent. It went steaming northward on the seas. It rushed to Alaska and to the Klondike. It carried Soapy Smith and his band of expert thieves to Skagway, at the foot of the White Pass.

6

White pass

Skagway is a town built near the end of the inland waterway called the Lynn Canal. It is in the upper panhandle coastal section of Alaska. Here the towering mountains point snowy peaks toward the sky. Here, on their craggy sides, blue glaciers cling—great seas of ice in constant slow motion. When the water of the Lynn Canal is calm, these giants cast their reflections on it. Until 1896 only the Indians knew this country well. Very few white men had made their way over the mountains by the only two trails that led to the interior. These were the White and the Chilkoot passes.

Old Capt'n Moore was one of the men who knew the passes. He was a tough ex-sailor who had lived in Alaska and the Yukon country for nearly ten years. He was tough enough to carry mail by dog sled, and had crossed the passes in mid-winter. It was Capt'n Moore who, with the help of Carmack's friend Skookum Jim, had made the first survey of White Pass. He went to the flat land on the shore, where the Skagway River rushes down to join the sea, and, under the shadow of the mountains, laid claim to the land. Capt'n Moore built a house and a store, then brought in his wife and children. He thought that gradually a town would grow there. He thought that he would own it.

Skagway is an Indian word meaning "the home of the north wind." Yet the north wind was gentle there. It came down in a calmer spirit after it had swept over White Pass with an icy, killing blast.

Skagway wasn't really a town when the first ships arrived with the cheechacos. They dropped anchor out in deep water. Over the rails came boxes, bales, sleds, dogs, horses, flour sacks, tents, stoves, tools, canned goods—and men!

The small boats and barges hastily thrown together on shore to bring in this avalanche of howling, shrieking animals and men with their goods were not enough. Horses swam to shallow water, then floundered to shore. Dogs emerged dripping. Men, and a few hardy women, swam and then waded ashore. They ran about looking for their damaged boxes and crates. They put up tents and spent a few hurried days gathering up

43

their goods.

Then they started for the trail up White Pass, unaware of what lay ahead of them. Nobody had told them that the trail was going to be so difficult, and so terrible an experience, that they would be lucky to survive it. They were all happy to be on land again and "almost in the gold fields"—where they expected to gather up gold by the bushel like pebbles on a beach.

Overwhelmed by this sudden flood of excited humans and welter of material, Capt'n Moore stood aghast. What could he do? He owned

Skagway—or thought that he did. He had a legal claim to the land. Yet these frantic gold hunters paid no attention to his claim. He shrugged, and started to build a dock a mile long, out to deep water, hoping to cash in on the unloading problem.

As each day brought more ships from the States, more tents went up in Skagway. Shacks appeared too, as if by some kind of magic. Many of the new arrivals had plans for something besides digging in the dirt for gold. Rough log cabins became stores, and a restaurant hung out a sign painted on the seat of a pair of old pants. Shanties made of rickety boards pried from packing boxes were put up for saloons, a blacksmith shop, and a hotel. Some of them had false fronts on top—putting on style. The muddy main street was dubbed Broadway, and within a few short weeks it was a mass of men, horses, dogs, and even a few goats.

The newcomers starting up the pass thought that it wasn't going to be so difficult. Even a wagon could bump along on the first part of it. Then as the trail wound upward it got so narrow that it was only a slight path, and so steep that the climb winded many. It wound and turned abruptly around boulders in so crooked a fashion that it seemed to double back on itself. A man bent almost double under his pack didn't dare look down the cliffs into the gulches and gorges below. Some people fell over the edge. Their bodies caught on projecting rocks and just stayed there. Nobody had time to bring them up and bury them.

The line of cheechacos grew thick, until men were touching as they climbed. Horses too fell over the edge, and the path soon began to be called "Dead Horse Trail." Horses, oxen and mules scrambled along with the men, over rocks and sharp gravel, dying by the thousand on the way. The trail became littered with discarded baggage. And then snow began to fall. Before long the snow was packed down so hard that it rose like a high-built road. During that winter three thousand horses died on the trail over White Pass, or in the gulches.

In mid-winter, the Canadian Mounted Police took up residence at the top of the pass. This was the border of Canada. The Mounties made their own rules for the good of this horde of ignorant people, and they enforced them. If an animal arrived in serious condition, it was shot by a Mountie to relieve its suffering. If a man arrived without a minimum of five hundred dollars, he was sent back. If a cheechaco didn't have enough provisions for a year in that country where food was so hard to come by, he had to go back to Skagway. And the Canadian authorities had the Mounties collect duty from Americans on their goods.

After a while the pass was so cluttered with trunks, dead animals, and supplies thrown from the backs of suffering men, that it was not possible to use it. The trail was closed. Then a man from Minnesota named George Brackett hired workers and cleared it. They improved it enough so that the line of men and animals could begin moving again. Even when the cold went down to sixty below zero, desperate men struggled up the trail. Their eyes looked crazed with the gold fever that they could not control. Among them was a man from Chicago who was painfully leading his horse.

"I'm going to be one of the first over. I'll get

there in time. I'll go home with sacks full of nuggets as big as my fist." But he couldn't bend his half-frozen fingers into a fist—and the gold was a dream that was fast becoming a nightmare.

Along the trail was a herd of two thousand cattle that had been driven up from New Mexico. With the cattle the cowhands drove a herd of sheep and sixty horses. And they brought forty lumbermen to build boats. These cowhands had never expected to ride herd on a tossing little ship and then struggle up a high, narrow pass through deep snow. But they did it! They brought most of the livestock safely down to the shores of Lake Bennet. Here they put the lumberjacks to cutting timber and building scows. Then they spent the rest of the winter keeping wolves away from the sheep, taking care of the stock, and planning the long voyage down the Yukon to Dawson with their bawling, bleating herds.

Back in Skagway the town was booming. Capt'n Moore was furious, for the new surveyor, Frank Reid, said that his house was in the middle of a newly laid out street. Who was this Frank Reid, anyway, to tell Capt'n Moore to move his house? Reid had been a soldier in the western Indian battles, and then a schoolteacher. Now he was a new resident of Skagway. Capt'n Moore took his case to the law, and several years later, long after he had moved his house to another spot, he won it.

Down Broadway moved a packed, jammed

mass of men, wagons and animals. Indians were there, too, earning high fees as expert packers for those about to go over the pass. Men stopped long enough to watch a Russian in a red tunic and fur cap put his performing bear through its act. Capt'n Moore's small granddaughter drove along in a wagon pulled by a tame moose. On the rattling plank sidewalks men sold balloons, boots, gold pans, and blanket coats. Every few feet there seemed to be a fellow with a tray and on it three small walnut shells and a rubber pea.

"Say, look at him! Bet I can guess under what shell that pea goes. Sure—I'll bet five dollars."

The cheechaco was robbed in saloons, in dance halls, in stores, and even by a smooth-talking, soft-spoken man who said he was a preacher taking up a collection for his church. This was the "Reverend" Charles Bowers, one of Soapy's men.

A cheechaco struggling up the muddy beach with his goods was hailed by a reporter. "Where you from? Abilene? Why, that's my home town. Shake hands, friend. Now tell me—do you need packers for the pass? How much money do you have with you? Want to buy a fine horse?"

If the cheechaco from Abilene was able to get over White Pass after that with enough goods and enough money to pass the Mounties, he was lucky. The "reporter" was a bunco man and, like the "Reverend" and many of the storekeepers as well, he was one of Soapy Smith's gang.

Nobody could tell, on arrival, who was honest and who wasn't. Soapy knew, all right. Soapy Smith was in control. Soapy preferred his real name, Jefferson Randolph Smith, to his nickname. He looked like a Southern gentleman, and he spoke like one. But his gentlemanly qualities were all in his soft voice, his well-dressed person, and his courteous manner.

Soapy controlled some of the politicians of Skagway through bribery. He had a large, well-organized group of gunmen and thugs who could hold a threat of death over everybody resisting them. He had secret spies in every business. They all reported to Soapy and turned a share of their ill-gotten money over to him. He was wealthy and powerful in a very short time, before the people of Skagway realized that he was in control.

In Skagway there was no law. And the Canadian Mounties were across the border and at the top of the passes, where they were ready for Soapy's men if they tried to cross. Skagway became the toughest town on the North American continent. If a person who had been swindled drew his pistol to defend himself he was shot down in cold blood. All of Soapy's men had come from the worst gun-slinging towns in the American West.

In Skagway the cemetery was a Boot Hill, and men were buried there with their boots on every day. The undertaker made a good profit after he had paid a share to Soapy. There seemed to be nothing going on in town that Soapy didn't have a share in. And yet he was such a pleasant, smiling man! And he was so charitable!

"Parson," he said to a minister whose flock needed a church, "I'll give you the money to start your church fund if you will raise the rest of it."

The fund was raised, and then the minister was robbed. "That's a shame, Parson," said Soapy. The minister knew that all of the money was in Soapy's big trunk in his office. But what could anybody do about it? When Soapy had Skagway under his control he sent some of his best men to Dyea, to rob cheechacos on the Chilkoot Pass trail.

7

In deadly snows

A ship nosed its way into Dyea Inlet among a mass of craft made up of every known kind of vessel. A young man leaning eagerly over the rail, pressed on both sides by the jam of passengers, wondered how most of these ships had ever survived the voyage along the Pacific Coast. The blue water reflected towering peaks capped with snow. Glaciers looked as if they might slide down at any moment on the cluster of tents, shacks and false-fronted cabins. It was magnificent scenery, but who looked at it?

Dogs howled. Horses neighed in panic as they were dropped into the water from boxes swung out from ships' decks. Bales and bags were tossed on the beach. Men shouted and swore, and scrambled about in confusion. This was the doorstep to Chilkoot Pass, up there against the sky, where the mountains were scooped out like a saddle.

Snow was falling in thick flakes as soft and dry as feathers. Perched three miles farther north along the shore, where a rushing river came down from the glaciers, the town of Dyea was a twin to Skagway. Chilkoot Pass looked impossible to climb when a man was loaded with supplies and equipment. It was six hundred feet higher than White Pass, but shorter by ten miles.

Here pack animals could go only part way on the dizzy, frozen climb. Yet during the winters of 1897 and 1898 more than twenty thousand men and women made their hard way over it. As on White Pass, Mounties arrived in the winter to police the Canadian boundary. And every cheechaco had to carry a year's supply of food and clothing and tools in with him, and have five hundred dollars in money.

By April some of these bearded, dirty men had been on the Dyea side of the pass for three or four months. They moved slowly up and down, hauling their tons of goods, a hundred pounds at a time, over the dizzy climb to the top. Indian packers, both men and women, with tump-lines tied around their foreheads, made the trip loaded until they were bent double. These Indians were of three tribes—the Chilkoots, the Tlingits and the Chilkats. They were making more money than they had ever seen before.

The young man, Jack London by name, who had leaned on the ship's railing with such eagerness, was both alert and tough. His sixty-year-old companion, a relative named Shephard, was neither. Jack London did not wait for his goods to be dumped from the smaller boats carrying goods to the shore. He sprang into the shallow water and pulled them out himself. He didn't need an Indian packer. In any case he did not have enough money to afford one. The packers were becoming difficult. They kept raising their prices along the trail, and refused to work on Sunday. Most of them were Presbyterians, converted long since by missionaries.

The snow-covered town was a roaring frontier settlement. The street was churned into black, snowy mush by men, horses, oxen and dogs. Jack had made three friends on shipboard and the four prepared to move up the pass at once. Shephard, however, lost heart completely; he sold his outfit and booked passage back to San Francisco on the *Umatillo*, the ship that had brought him.

But Jack London was out for adventure more than for gold. Only twenty years old, he had already been a smuggler with his own boat on San Francisco Bay. Then he had joined the harbor police and chased smugglers. Then he had become a tramp, riding the rails across country. After that he went to college for a while. Now he wanted to be a writer.

The four friends joined a mob of sweating men

54

on the way to the pass. The first leg of the trip was not difficult. "What do they mean, back-breaking?" one of Jack's friends said. "They must be soft. I could do this every day. Drop out? Not me." Men on the trail laughed, and joked about how tough they were. They were still on the wagon ruts, passing between snow-laden trees.

The trail crossed the frozen river several times as it wound along. It grew steeper, more difficult. After a while Jack began to notice telltale signs of the trail's getting worse. Trunks were dumped beside the trail, along with furniture and tools. Things were getting heavy on the bent backs of men and horses. Some prospectors were even throwing away their rubber boots.

"What's he doing?" asked a curious stampeder.

A man was gathering up the discarded boots and stuffing them into sacks. A sourdough laughed over his shoulder. "He takes them down to Juneau and sells them again to more chee-chacos. The same boots arrive over and over in the dump heaps on the passes."

The next part of the trail was a steep one. From Finnegan's Camp, which was a tent res-taurant and a blacksmith shop, they had to make their way over boulders and roots of trees along a narrow canyon of the river. Here they moved in single file. Animals strained under the loads into what was called Canyon City. This was a jumble of shacks and saloons set in a gloomy

gorge. At the far end they came to Pleasant
Camp, a camp similar to Canyon City but outside
of the gorge.

Next came Sheep Camp. This was a noisy, con-
fused place where dirty tents covered every inch
of ground. Here a tent hotel, in which men slept
on the floor, coined money.

Jack craned his head back and could scarcely
believe the sight that met his eyes. Straight up
the steep mountain there was what looked like a
long, thin snake crawling slowly over ice and

snow. It was a chain of human beings. As they went, the climbers moved over snow packed so hard that, within an hour, a fresh fall felt like stone underfoot.

Jack London could carry a load as heavy as one hauled by an Indian packer. But others couldn't. Most had to drop out of line at the foot of the mountain and rest at a place called the Scales. Here goods were weighed again, and the Indian packers raised their prices.

This was the end of the trail for animals and for sleds. From this point a man with dogs had to carry each one on his back to the top. Then he must return for the others. All winter, in the darkness of day as well as by night, the long chain moved upwards. Beside it another line moved back down. Few could get their goods over the pass in less than three months.

This line of men went up in a strange, bent-over gait called "the Chilkoot lock-step." To the summit of the pass it was four miles from Sheep Camp, where every night an average of fifteen hundred people slept, waiting their turn to go up and come down. At one place the mountain was covered with solid ice. Here some fellows had cut out steps. Then they charged the cheechacos a toll to use them. But despite such extra difficulties, up they went, in storms, in blinding sunlight, and in the darkness of night. The lines never stopped, except for a day or two in a raging blizzard.

"Move along, men!"

At the top, a "Yellow-leg" or Mountie, nick-named for the stripes on his trousers, stood ready to inspect them. Up here at the home of the north wind, a few Mounties lived in a small hut. Nobody could understand how they survived. One of them had to be on duty all the time, day and night, to shovel the hut's doors and windows free of falling snow and thus prevent those sleeping inside from smothering. They had only a small stove and some bunks. They were frost-bitten, and often ill with bronchitis. Yet they mounted guard and saw to it that no man or woman went into Canada without a ton of goods and five hundred dollars.

There were two kinds of people crossing the Chilkoot. Cheechacos hungry for gold had a fever-ish look in their eyes. Others were going in to get the gold from the cheechacos. Some did it by cheating the ignorant, or running bunco gambling games even on the snow. Soapy Smith sent some of his smooth operators to disguise themselves as cheechacos on the Chilkoot trail. At each stop-ping place they got out their little walnut shells and the rubber pea. They raked in the money, always taking a share back to Skagway and Soapy.

Many were going in with goods for sale. There was a man with a big box of cats and kittens. They were intended to be sold to lonely miners for pets. There was a man with a crate of eggs on his back. There was a stocky woman pulling a sled with a hot stove on it. She would start a bakery, and keep herself provided with hot meals on the way. And there was a widow from Tombstone, Arizona, with a load of brooms tied on her back. Some men had bundles of plumed hats, or sacks of flour, or turkeys, plows, dishes, beans, or even a couple of timbers on their backs.

A couple named Goddard made trips up and down over Chilkoot Pass all winter and spring. Piece by piece they brought over a small steamboat.

During the winter a long rope tramway, wound around a wheel and turned by a gasoline motor, was set up to get goods up the mountain. But most of it went in on the backs of the thousands of people who crossed Chilkoot Pass that winter and spring. They came from everywhere—Arabia, Germany, England, Canada, China and Turkey. Most of them, however, were Americans. Most of them were young and vigorous men. But there were a few women, and a few older people.

At the top of the pass each man made a pile of his goods. Then he left it and went back for more. There was little robbery. In that country the worst possible crime, by common consent, was theft. In American territory a miners' meeting handed out rough justice to a thief. And in Canada the Mounties always got their man! A thief would be hanged, or whipped, or run out into below-freezing weather. Not many were ready to take the risk. But there were other risks they did take.

The September before, the frantic men toiling up the pass could see, when they turned their heads, a huge glacier hanging far up on the mountain. Suddenly the weather turned unusually warm. Men threw off coats and boots. Nobody had time to notice the glittering sun rays reflected on the ice in blue, pink, green and yellow. Nobody had time to bother with the warnings sent out by the mass of ice clinging to the mountainside. Loud reports and thunderous roars came from the glacier as it cracked and slipped on the rocky slopes, and the warm sun formed a growing pool of water inside its gleaming surface.

The Indians knew what it meant. They warned, "No stay on mountain. No good—no good." Their eyes were frightened. Some of the old-timers listened, and left the mountainsides with the Indians. But many of the cheechacos didn't.

When the glacier broke, those sleeping in tents along the trail thought that the end of the world had come. The sound was that of a thousand cannons belching fury. The cheechacos leaped to their feet and ran, stumbling over the rocks beside the fast little stream. Then one turned and screamed. A wall of water twenty feet high was sweeping through the gorge. It caught the men and women and tossed them to destruction.

But by April the hordes of newcomers had forgotten, if indeed they had heard, the story of the melting glacier. The trail was choked with men and goods. When a late snow came down in a thick wet blanket, the Indians again gave warning, and left. Again they said urgently, "No go up. No good up." Snow high up was melting. The several hundred cheechacos there only laughed, or shrugged. Up at the Scales, Joppe and Mueller, two men who ran a tent restaurant there, went to bed without worrying. They were awakened by a shout:

"Help! Help! Come help us."

They leaped up, dressing hurriedly, and went out to find that a snowslide had come down and covered several tents. Digging as fast as their cold hands could work, the rescuers managed to take everybody out alive except three people.

"More slides are coming," someone shouted. "Get out! Everybody get out fast!"

The two hundred men and women grabbed a long rope that was fastened along the ravine and started down. Now it was thin daylight, ghostly on the snow. They slipped and slid down as the morning advanced.

Like the blast of a thousand sticks of dynamite an avalanche of snow roared down the mountain and dropped on the two hundred fleeing cheechacos. Joppe and Mueller were two of them.

As if by magic hundreds of men came up the difficult slope to dig frantically into the thirty feet of wet snow. Three hours later Mueller was taken out, miraculously still breathing. He had lain there, unable to move a finger under the weight of the slide, but able to hear other victims crying and praying. One of the rescuers was Vernie Woodward, Joppe's sweetheart. She had been packing her own goods farther down the pass, and had heard the news in Sheep Camp. When Joppe's limp form was pulled from the snow she flung herself on him, working his arms, breathing into his mouth.

The others tried to pull her away. "He's dead, Vernie. You can't help him."

But Vernie wouldn't give up. Suddenly Joppe opened his eyes and said in a weak voice, "Hello, Vernie."

The story went up and down the trail. "Did you hear how Vernie brought her fellow to life?" In Skagway, in Dyea, over White Pass, and over the Chilkoot, all the way to the lakes, everybody talked about Vernie, the heroine of the big avalanche.

8

The mounties meet Soapy

Superintendent Sam Steele left the guarding of the passes to some of his men, and brought his headquarters to Lake Bennett. He sat at his small table, a deep frown on his face. In the safe in his tiny cabin on the lake shore he had a great deal of money that had been collected in Canadian duties from the stampeders. There was no way of getting it to Ottawa except by way of Alaska, and Alaska had neither law nor order. He thought of his few troopers. Most of them were Englishmen, younger sons of well-to-do families. They were men who were adventurous, and yet calm. They believed so firmly in the law that they usually had no trouble in maintaining it with quiet voice and without drawing their weapons. Somehow these Mounted Policemen carried authority with them, and they seldom had to give an order twice. The most lawless men listened and obeyed. They all knew that Sam Steele and his troopers would do exactly what they said they would do.

Steele thought over his list of courageous young men. There were a few Americans among them. One of these was Inspector Zachary Taylor Wood, a grandson of the Zachary Taylor who had been President of the United States. Steele sent for Inspector Wood.

When the young Mountie stood before him in his scarlet jacket and yellow striped breeches, Steele leaned back in his chair and said, "Wood, you know that we have collected more than a hundred and fifty thousand dollars this winter at the two passes. Now this money must be taken to Ottawa. The question is, how do we get by Soapy Smith?"

Inspector Wood nodded. "It can't go over White Pass and through Skagway, that's obvious. Soapy has the town completely in his control."

"We've got to go through American territory to reach our ship," replied the Superintendent, frowning. "I have picked you for this job, Inspector. Do you have any suggestions?" He motioned with his hand. "Sit down."

The Mountie sat stiffly beside the table covered with piles of papers and letters. "The only other way out is over the Chilkoot to Dyea," he said. "But that's not much better than Skagway. Once we get across the border Soapy's men are sure

to be waiting. It is no secret that we have a fortune in tax. money to take out."

Together they worked out a plan. Inspector Wood spread word that he was being transferred back to the Calgary area. He would leave the following week by way of Chilkoot Pass, taking only his personal baggage.

The day of departure was bright, with a pale late-spring sun gleaming on the snow. Inspector Wood left his barracks cabin accompanied by several other constables carrying his bags. The camp was just stirring. The stampeders still camped around the lake were building up fires in their tents and shacks. Curls of smoke rose lazily into the air. There was a scent of frying bacon and flapjacks.

Already a number of the prospectors were bringing in the morning supply of firewood, or getting out their saws for boat building. They stopped to stare curiously at the knot of men in front of the barracks. Constables were loading Inspector Wood's bags on a sled, and they were having some trouble. The bags were so heavy that it took four men to carry each one. Two of the stampeders nodded at each other, and hurried indoors. Within minutes they came out wearing their mackinaw coats and sun goggles. They disappeared up the trail well in advance of the Inspector, his four troopers and their overloaded sled.

The going was difficult on the trail at this time of year under the best of circumstances. Pulling a heavily loaded sled up through melting slush, and then down on soft snow and ice, was an almost impossible task. But the constables were men who had muscles as strong as their determination.

At Dyea there was a curious crowd at the docks. Men stared at the bags carried by four constables and placed carefully in a small boat. Inspector Wood was not surprised that there were several fellows in the throng who watched the loading into the boat with broad grins on their unshaven faces. Holsters were slung low on their hips, and hats were cocked over their faces. It was easy enough to recognize them as Soapy's gunmen. The Inspector watched them carefully, wondering when they would make their move, and what it would be.

Inspector Wood sighed with relief as his small launch swung away from the dock. Then he saw the gunmen jump into another launch. It started with a sputtering roar, and followed the Mounties' launch. The constables kept their hands on their weapons. Their launch gained speed. Far up ahead Inspector Wood could see a column of black smoke from the stack of the *Tartar*, the ship that was to take him, with his heavy baggage, to Victoria, British Columbia. It was waiting at the long Skagway wharf. At this moment it seemed unlikely that he would ever reach its decks.

The launch following him was a fast one. It moved along with a trail of white foam behind it. It was already more than close enough for a good pistol shot, and it was coming closer. The man handling the motor pushed his hat back and laughed, his reddish beard glistening in the sun. Inspector Wood drew his gun and stood at the rail, waiting. Just as the other boat came abreast of him, it made a sudden sharp turn and headed straight for the Mounties' launch. It was going to try to ram them! Wood cried out and the Mounties' helmsman swung his boat off course just in time. The constables put on full steam, and the other boat made no further effort to overtake them. Inspector Wood still kept his pistol cocked.

Now he could clearly see the long wharf at Skagway. At the end, where the *Tartar* was tied up, sailors with loaded rifles stood guarding the gangway. At the wharf entrance there was an ominous crowd of men with pistols at their hips. In front of this group a figure dressed in a fine black suit stood out against the slovenly outfits of his men. The launch came to rest against the wharf, and the constables got out with their valuable baggage.

The man in the black suit, Soapy Smith, called out to Inspector Wood, "Come to Skagway and be my guest! We'll give you a good time here."

The Inspector looked at him grimly, and followed the gold on board ship. The sailors backed up the gangway, rifles leveled at the gunmen. The ship moved out into deep water. Soapy shrugged off his failure, and went back to his plundering of the ignorant prospectors.

9

The strangest fleet in the world

Down below the far slopes of the passes, on the Canadian side, the shores of Lake Bennett and Lake Lindemann were crowded with thousands of tents. A Mountie stood outside his headquarters and looked grimly up at the trail from Chilkoot. Boxes, bales and sleds were bouncing and rolling down the white slope. Men were yelling with joy at the relief they felt in getting over the pass.

"Whoopee! Yaaaaay!"

Down they came, sliding like toboggans, rolling over and over in the snow. There was always a long line of them pulling into tent city. More tents went up every day. The Mountie glanced at his watch, and began his inspection rounds.

He took a look at blacksmith shops, restaurant-tents, and saloons. "Get those dogs out of harness," he called to a man who had left his team of malamutes standing too long, with the result that the dogs were tangled up and fighting.

Farther along the Mountie pulled two fighting stampeders apart. One yelled, "I'm going to kill him. We ain't partners any longer. How are we going to divide our gear?"

The Inspector separated the gear into two equal piles and tossed a coin to decide which of the men should choose first. The ex-partners gathered up their shares to go their separate ways.

Next the Mountie noticed several men working on one of the hundreds of boats, rafts, and scows in various stages of construction. This one was nothing but a floating crate. It would leak like a sieve. "Boys, you have to do better than that," the Mountie warned. "You'll sink her before you get on the Yukon. Calk her up!"

Some men were out in the forest cutting trees. Others were hauling their lumber into camp, usually pulling it themselves by means of ropes tied on their shoulders. Others were whipsawing the logs into planks on scaffolds built up off the ground.

The Mountie stayed longest at the saw-pits, for there tempers were hottest. One partner had to stand on top, sawing with the long two-man saw. The other was below, guiding the lower end of the saw. The man below got the worst of it, for sawdust came down into his eyes, and if he closed them a moment the saw slipped out of the cut. When that happened, the man above went into a wild rage. And if the man above was a little careless with his saw, the one beneath was ready to fight it out with him. The job of whip-sawing heavy green logs into lumber was tough enough to break up almost any partnership. Yet every vessel had to be made that way.

The Mountie stopped for a few moments to speak to an old Dutch woman, as straight as a tree trunk, who was trying to build her own raft. He looked at the crate of squalling cats and mewing kittens, nodding in relief to find that they were being fed regularly. He watched the Goddards putting their steam launch together.

These campers looked like some strange race never before seen on earth. Men wore thick beards to keep them warm and protect their chins from frostbite. Men and women alike blacked their faces with a mixture of charcoal and oil to keep the snow glare from burning their skins to blisters. They fastened on handmade wooden eye protectors, to prevent snow blindness.

Like the others, Jack London and his three friends finally got their eight thousand pounds of gear and food to Lake Lindemann. There they began to construct their boats. One of the friends, a carpenter named Sloper, set up a rough sawmill eight miles from the lake and cut the lumber for their boats. He added to their store of money by cutting for others as well. Jack, the sailor of the crowd, designed two small boats. He wrote a poem for each, and called the boats *The Yukon Belle* and *The Belle of the Yukon*. Then he cut and sewed into sails the canvas tents that he and his friends owned. He had everything in shipshape condition, ready for the time when the ice would break.

With the coming of spring in May, snow melted and ran rivers across the earth, flooding tents and making mud of the ground. Then a carpet of wildflowers bloomed on shore, and the lake ice melted into slush and soon became blue water. Thirty thousand stampeders were waiting for the Yukon ice to break so they could float down to Dawson. On the edges of the two lakes, canoes, rafts, barges—boats of every kind and size—were loaded with thousands of tons of food, tools and articles for sale.

A couple of Mounties went to the big river to see what its condition was. They came back to report that the river ice had broken with a roar and a sudden rush of clear water. The stampeders could sail.

At one end of the lake cowpunchers from New Mexico herded their cattle and sheep to the shore. For two months the herd had been penned inside a corral made of high-packed snow in order to keep wolves out. Now cows bawled and sheep bleated as they were driven onto scows. The cowboys gave a series of "Yippees!" and pushed off. This was May 29, 1898.

Two women hoisted a sail made of their long

petticoats and sang "Onward Christian Soldiers" as they shoved their boat from shore.

Other sails were raised. They were made of everything including rugs, blankets, and tent canvas. The advance fleet of this armada sailed out under a light breeze, headed toward the series of lakes leading into the mighty Yukon. They didn't know what they faced. But they were happy.

All across the water men began to sing. Their voices blended in different tunes, different words, and somehow made one song of the sound. This was a song of triumph—of freedom from the snows! It was a song of work done, of hardships overcome, of a golden fortune waiting. Soon the little vessels disappeared, and another fleet prepared to depart at dawn.

The Yukon Belle and *The Belle of the Yukon*, two men in one, three in the other, did not start out for the river with the first day's crowd. But a few days later they joined the huge flotilla that was moving along and covering the green lake water with the strangest collection of boats that ever sailed.

The advance fleet reached the first rapids and found a jam of major proportions. Here the waters poured into a canyon and, rushing between high stone cliffs, formed a giant, spinning whirlpool.

The cheechacos lined up along the banks and looked at the whirlpool in terror. An old sourdough who knew the country was preparing to portage down around it by walking. As he packed his stuff on his back, he said, "Three years ago a couple of boys got caught in that whirlpool. Their boat spun around and around it for six hours before they got her out. I tell you, those boys were dizzy. Yes-siree, they were just plain tuckered out."

Here hundreds of craft were pulled up, their owners afraid to venture farther. Beyond the whirlpool there were two rapids where the rushing torrent of water dashed madly over the rocks, throwing white spray high into the air. First came the Squaw Rapids. Then below that was the terrible White Horse Rapids, so named because the foam looked like white ponies leaping about.

Jack London and his three companions edged through the craft jammed above Miles Canyon with its whirlpool. On the shore stood a Mountie, Chief Inspector Sam Steele. He had come down from the summit of the Pass to take charge. He knew that most of these stampeders had never handled a boat before, and that many of the boats were not seaworthy anyway. All along the banks below the rapids there were wrecks of some of the first boats that tried to go through, and already some men had drowned. Inspector Steele delivered a stern talk to those gathering in ever greater numbers above the rapids.

"People say that the Mounted Police make the laws as they go along. I am making some now. Corporal Dixson will take charge here, and he will not permit a boat through the canyon unless it is steered by competent men, and unless it is so made that it can make the voyage. Women and children must walk around the rapids."

The gold hunters looked at each other in despair. London's friends shook their heads. There

were nearly a thousand boats along the shores above the canyon and the rapids.

"We can't make it," Sloper said. "What do you think, Jack?"

Jack swung around and walked down to look at the rapids.

"There is nothing to it," he said. "Instead of trying to avoid the rocks by fighting the current, we will just go with the current."

He fastened the sail tightly over the provisions,

placed his men in the first boat, and pushed out into the canyon. A roar went up from the men on shore.

"Look at him go! Two to one he can't make it."

"I'll take you up on that."

The boat shot into the canyon. It whirled about in the whirlpool, and came out again. Then it rode the rapids, around the rocks and over them, and came safely into calm water below. There the men got out and walked back upstream. Then they brought down the second boat without trouble. Cheechacos swarmed around Jack and begged him to steer them down. London, who could not pass up a chance to make some money when he had so little, decided to stay for a while and take boats down at twenty-five dollars a trip.

His friends took one of the boats, and sailed off downriver without him. Jack shrugged, sorry for a moment that he had decided to stay. Then he began to pocket his fees, and told himself that this was probably a lot more than he would find in the diggings. He wasn't one of the feverish prospectors who believed all the stories printed in the States. Jack London wasn't quite sure why he was there, anyway. But one thing he did know. This life was full of adventure and excitement. He was learning a lot, and enjoying it, and that was enough.

On to Dawson

The Klondike! The Klondike! "How do I get to the Klondike?"

They swarmed over White Pass, down to Lake Bennett. They made an endless line moving in the Chilkoot lock-step over that pass and down to Lake Lindemann. But there was still another route by ship all the way to the mouth of the Yukon River.

"This way it costs more," a young man from Alabama said. "But I can get there without walking a step. I'm not climbing over those high passes in the mountains. Not me! I'm going to ride a ship right up the Pacific into Bering Sea. Then they say I can get on a river steamer, go up the Yukon, and get off right in Dawson City. That's the route for me."

It sounded so easy to the young fellow from Alabama who was traveling with his two hound dogs. It seemed the best route to the college professors, lawyers, and doctors who were also on board. They were all young and vigorous. They all wanted to pick up the gold and get back home so they could continue with their careers. On shipboard they gathered together and talked about politics, religion, philosophy and the arts. When they weren't discussing these subjects they tried, lying on the crowded decks, to eat and sleep. It was August, 1897.

The Yukon River route seemed especially wonderful to the owner of the ship, Mr. W. D. Wood. He had been the Mayor of Seattle, but he happened to be in San Francisco when the *Excelsior* steamed in loaded with gold. The excitement caught him suddenly. He telegraphed his resignation to Seattle. He arranged for money. He rushed down and bought a ship called the *Humboldt*, and had her outfitted to sail to the Yukon River in Bering Sea. He didn't even go home to Seattle before sailing.

Loaded with baggage, stampeders crowded on board the *Humboldt*. In the excitement, far too many were sold passage. They milled around, well past the hour of departure, and still the ship didn't sail. Wood was frantic when the captain found him.

"What's wrong?" Mr. Wood asked.

"She can't sail, Mr. Wood. She's badly overloaded. We'll have to take off nearly forty thousand pounds of baggage."

"All right. Then take it off. Unload!"

When the jammed-up passengers saw a lot of their baggage being unloaded they yelled and howled. Some drew pistols and others got out shotguns. They rushed to find the owner.

"Where's Wood? Hang him! Hang him!"

The captain and his crew leaped into the riot, and police arrived in time to quiet the passengers. Some agreed to wait for another ship, accepted a refund and left peaceably. The baggage was sorted out. Then, with passengers crushed together on deck, and people shouting and cheering on the dock, the *Humboldt* sailed.

The voyage was long and rough, and by the time they reached the mouth of the Yukon most of the passengers were too ill and weak to care much where they were. However, at sight of the gray waters of the Yukon pouring into the cold sea, they revived.

"Where's the boat to take us upriver?" they wanted to know.

Nothing was visible to the men on the *Humboldt* but a blue sky, gray waters, and low land that was treeless and desolate. Mr. Wood, pale with worry, had to tell them that there was no river boat. The men were indignant. How were they to get up the Yukon? From here it was seventeen hundred miles to the Klondike. Mr. Wood was forced to admit that he was counting on building a small steamboat, and that he had brought the necessary materials and machinery with him on the *Humboldt*. At this news the men became really angry and Wood thought that he was going to be hanged or shot on the spot. But the cooler heads among the passengers saw that they could not get to the Klondike by executing their leader, even though it would have given them a lot of pleasure to do it.

With no alternative, then, they went ashore, unloaded the vessel themselves, and pitched their tents near by. Another ship from the States soon hove to and unloaded its cargo of gold seekers. They too had to build a boat to get them upriver.

Mr. Wood had had enough trouble with his passengers. All he wanted now was to get away. But when he tried to go home on the departing ocean vessel, he was caught and held captive till the boat was out of sight. It took his hard-working passengers three weeks to build their river boat. When it was done they decided that it resembled nothing so much as an Eskimo boot, and so they dubbed it *The Mukluk*, although its official name was *The Seattle No. 1*.

The other group constructed a little boat called the *May West*. In September both tiny steamers started chugging up the Yukon although the passengers knew the freeze-up was near. They hoped to make it. They didn't. The ice came suddenly, and caught them halfway to the Klon-

dike. The unlucky passengers of both vessels went
ashore, put together shacks or pitched tents, and
went into winter quarters. *Humboldt* stampeders
called their town "Suckerville," and nobody
allowed Mayor Wood to forget that he was
responsible for their situation. They were still
eight hundred miles from Dawson.

Mayor Wood added to his unpopularity by
refusing to sell provisions that he was trying to
take to Dawson for sale. The stampeders had a
meeting—and he agreed to sell. Then he managed
to fill a pack with food, put it on his back, and
start out on foot in the snow. After trudging
overland for nine hundred miles he reached St.
Michaels, the old Russian port near the mouth
of the Yukon.

When he got there he saw a fleet of queer, leaky ships of different sizes unloading more "suckers." They came ashore expecting to step onto a fine river boat for the trip to Dawson. Many of them took a quick look at the wilderness and went back home on the same ships that had brought them. Mayor Wood went with them.

Many of those who stayed died in St. Michaels that winter, or in "Suckerville" halfway up the Yukon. A half-frozen fellow from Alabama appeared in St. Michaels to board ship for home. He was leading two shivering hounds.

And yet some stampeders did manage to reach the sourdough mining camp of Rampart City, a hundred miles up the river at the entrance to Minook Creek. There an Indian called Minook had found gold several years before, and started a rush.

One party had bought a little river boat, the *St. Michael*, from a Catholic Mission. The men who owned and manned the ship were all landlubbers, and had never sailed a ship. Most of them were teachers, salesmen, clerks, lawyers and doctors. It was autumn, just before freeze-up. They took the *St. Michael* as far as Rampart City, where their wood gave out. Then someone found coal in the rocks near the shack-town, and the crew set to and dug out enough coal to fuel the tiny boat.

As they steamed slowly toward Circle City, they saw that down the river there was a strange collection of craft coming toward them—canoes, rafts, boats, and a small steamboat. Why were they sailing *away* from Circle City?

"What's up?" The *St. Michael* hailed a boat crowded with bearded miners. "You're going the wrong way!"

"You'll find out if you get to Dawson. Starvation, that's what! Not enough food in Dawson to feed those left there. We're getting out."

The *St. Michael* continued up the river. Gold fever had become a wild, unreasoning urge to get to Dawson. Not far out of Circle, however, the little steamboat manned by landlubbers ran onto a sandbar. The passengers went ashore and tried desperately to figure out some way of getting to Dawson. Snow fell. The river freeze-up came suddenly. Men holed up in tents and shacks for the winter. They dreamed of Dawson, and the golden dust and nuggets lying around in the diggings.

In Dawson City people thought, "Any day now, before freeze-up, we'll see a ship or two come in loaded with food." No ship arrived. Constantine, of the Mounted Police, sent word to the Canadian Parliament in Ottawa that unless food could be gotten in many miners were going to starve before spring.

While one crowd of stampeders was straining every muscle to get to Dawson, another crowd of miners was trying desperately to get out of it. All that winter—in lonely cabins in the snows— miners died of starvation, even as stampeders were pouring painfully over the high passes to reach the Klondike. That winter the wandering caribou herds could not be found; and Indians and Eskimos depended on the caribou herds. Moose seemed unusually scarce. The great black and brown bears hibernated. Wolves howled around cabins, and dogs ate anything, even pieces of leather. The Mounties drew in their belts, and

went on half rations.

In Dawson nobody did die of starvation, after all. But the Indians suffered, for all the supplies were sold to the white men, and not to them. In the Indian camp at Moosehide many died from hunger that winter.

The Canadian government made plans to send help, but the help that they sent didn't reach Dawson until spring. Meanwhile the American Congress, after hearing a plea for aid for the miners in the north, arranged for five hundred reindeer to be shipped from Norway to the point on the Lynn Canal where Jack Dalton's trail started. (Dalton was an American frontiersman who cut a trail in from Pyramid Harbor in Alaska to Fort Selkirk in the Canadian Yukon. He charged a toll for the use of a trail that was almost impassable.) Laplanders were engaged to bring in the herd.

The herd reached Dalton trail in May of 1898. The trail was so rough that many deer died of falls along the way. There was no reindeer moss for them to eat, and more died for lack of food. By the time the Laplanders reached Dawson, they had only one hundred and fourteen reindeer with them. They had brought the herd over a wilderness trail seven hundred and fifty miles long. They straggled into Dawson in January, 1899. They had been on the trail nine months.

11

Through the wilderness

"The backdoor to the Yukon! Go overland through Canada. Get you there before the ships arrive at Dawson. Take Canadian trails!"

Those advertisements were run in Canadian newspapers. Articles advising the Canadian overland routes appeared in Canadian magazines. Important people printed opinions on the subject. One man who claimed to be an explorer said that the overland route through the Canadian Northwest was the only easy one. "Nothing to it. A good trail all the way," he said.

There were several overland routes, each recommended by a different group of backers. The two most popular were the Ashcroft Trail and the Peace River Trail from Edmonton. But there were some gold hunters who planned to go beyond the Peace River to Great Slave Lake and then down the Mackenzie River.

Stampeders got maps and studied them. "That trail from Ashcroft may be called the 'Long Trail' but it doesn't look so hard," one man told his partner. "It runs a thousand miles due north to the Klondike. We can do that, all right. Let's get going."

They poured into the tiny frontier town of Ashcroft by the thousand—Americans, Canadians, people from other countries. Objections that there might be difficulties were brushed aside.

"Why, don't you know that Western Union Telegraph Company men have been through here? They made the trail. We can just follow it."

By early spring in 1898 Ashcroft was churning with horses and wagons. There were more than a thousand men going that way, all sure that their horses would take them easily into Dawson. The first part of the trail led through forests. Clouds of mosquitoes and black flies came at them like billows of dark smoke. Men grabbed every available piece of cloth and covered their faces, necks, hands and legs. They could hardly breathe. These men from the cities did not know that with the melting snows insects take over the bush in the Canadian wilderness. Gradually through the summer they die off, until they are not a menace. But in the spring and early summer, in forested lands, insects can kill horses, blind bears, and drive men crazy.

On the Long Trail from Ashcroft horses and cattle died by the hundreds. Those who survived the insects often ate poisonous weeds, and died of that. Dead animals were left where they fell all along the trail. Wagons were abandoned. Men shouldered bulging packs and continued on foot.

"Where's that trail made by the Western Union men?" they wanted to know.

Before their swollen eyes there was soon no trail at all. What they had not been told was that the Western Union trail-blazers had quit after going only a short distance. The project for stringing telegraph wires into the Arctic regions had been abandoned.

A cheechaco pulled a newspaper out of his pocket and read one of the advertisements aloud: "The Ashcroft Trail is perfectly easy. A road gang has already gone up that way and made a good trail, even through regions until now impassable."

But there was no road gang. There had never been a road gang up there. That advertisement had been inserted by a man who owned a big store and wanted to sell clothing and tools to stampeders. As they walked farther and farther, men began to discard things—trunks, furniture, guitars, stoves, even a tin bathtub. Men grew so exhausted, and so desperate, that they threw away bulky coats and caps—every possible item that they thought they could do without. Tossed in the jumble of discarded things were photographs—often in gold frames—of wives and children, of sweethearts, of parents.

The men plodded on, as if crazed with the urge to get to the gold fields. Sometimes they stopped to carve messages on trees: "Where's that gold?" "Bury me here on the Long, Long Trail."

More than six hundred miles from Ashcroft, this route joined another coming in from the coast along the Stikine River. All during the winter of 1898 prospectors had been dragging sleds in over deep snows from a camp town called Glenora which was situated on the Stikine River. By spring much of this area was flooded and was nothing but a huge swamp. The gold seekers waded through miles of mud and shallow water. Two women in high boots and men's trousers and coats drove a herd of goats through the swamp and up onto the wilderness trail.

All that spring more stampeders came every day. One man, tied in the traces like a horse, was puffing and pulling a cart. There was another pushing a hand cart. Some just collapsed and died along the way with their animals. Others began to understand that they could never make it. They turned back. Many arrived in the roaring camp town of Wrangell, Alaska, and were soon robbed of any money that they had left. Soapy Smith had men in Wrangell, and they made of the town another Skagway for the cheechacos.

Through the Canadian wilds the stream of fortune-seekers moved slowly northward. It was a motley crowd. The widow of a Royal Canadian Mounted Policeman was on the trail with a loaded pistol. She was looking for the man who had murdered her husband. There were singers, black-faced minstrel comics, and a man with a barrel organ and a monkey.

An old miner with a grizzled gray beard shook his head in dismay and said to his partner, "I was on the trail to Californy when I was a little lad, with my father. I was twelve years old then, but I remember it all. It was nothing like this. This ain't a gold rush. It's a lot of crazy people. On the gold rush of '49 we were all men—no women. Look at that female over there ahead of us! She's got a load of satin dresses she's taking

to sell in the diggings at Dawson City. It's not making sense to me. And look at these entertainers! We are going to dig for gold. Not to sing and dance."

Up ahead there was a little circus parading gaily along. It had two painted wagons, a music box, and a striped tent in which a tightrope dancer would perform. This lady rode a sleek black horse with a white blaze on its forehead, and was followed by a troupe of performing dogs. The circus lasted until the rough and rushing Skeena River was reached. Then it turned around and tried to get home again.

At the same time, from Edmonton, in Alberta Province, thousands more were hitting the trail for the Peace River. They were excited by a flood of pamphlets, illustrated with maps, which described a road into the Klondike that would be open all winter. In the space of a few months the little frontier town of Edmonton had grown from about seven hundred people to five thousand. The town was a mass of tents and hastily thrown together shacks. It was packed with horses, men and women.

A large party of Englishmen started out with servants, bathtubs, bottles of champagne, and English grooms for their horses. Weeks later they straggled back into Edmonton. One had died of pneumonia, another had died of frostbite, and a servant had been attacked by the leader, who tried to knife him.

Everybody ran to the edge of town to watch a man from Chicago start out in a steam sleigh of his own invention. It was called the "I Will," and was guaranteed to slide over grass and bare ground as well as snow.

"She's got a locomotive," said one onlooker. "All loaded to go, and baggage on board."

"Bet it'll make ten miles an hour," another commented.

"She's off!" everybody yelled.

The "I Will" got up steam and, with the crowd cheering, made a rush into the mud—and sank. During the ensuing weeks the steam sleigh just rusted there, passed by the never-ending throng of stampeders. Among them there were some Kickapoo Medicine Show Indians. And there was another sleigh making a better take-off. It was drawn by a team of goats.

The strangest sights in the whole world came through Edmonton heading north through impassable forests and rivers. A man called Texas Smith brought along an invention which he called "The Duck." It had wheels made of wooden wine barrels so that it would roll easily over logs and boulders. But after five miles on the trail it burst its barrel wheels and fell apart.

Stampeders discovered, sooner or later, that the so-called trails weren't trails at all. To get to the Klondike by land they had to travel more than two thousand miles of some of the roughest country in the world. The ones who realized this before they had gone very far were lucky. They got back safely to their homes. A determined woman from Toronto, traveling with her husband and her brother, left a piano beside the trail, and turned back. All that the three wanted now was to go home.

Very few of those who started overland ever reached Dawson. One of those who did was Inspector Moodie of the Mounties. He was assigned to take a patrol and explore the route. After a trip lasting fourteen months, he arrived at Dawson, almost starving, in an Indian canoe.

Yet men and women pushed northward, refusing to listen to anybody who tried to discourage them. They tried to go down the Mackenzie River, where fierce Dog-rib Indians lived. They tried to cross Great Slave Lake in homemade boats, and were tossed about by huge waves and strong winds on this inland sea. Many drowned. They did not know that the Mackenzie was as wide as the Mississippi, that it emptied into the Arctic Ocean, and that it ran through country unexplored except by hardy Hudson Bay voyageurs in their long canoes. They attempted the unknown gorges of the Peel River and entered the land of the Crooked Eye Indians, who worshiped a cannibal god.

None of the men and women so gaily starting out overland ever found any gold. When winter caught them, some bunched together in hastily built cabins, calling these places Destruction City and Wind City. A few got through, somehow, to Dawson, only to go home on the next ship. They had been two years on the way. By then the gold rush was over in the Klondike. They did not even go out into the diggings. In 1899 a relief expedition was sent north from British Columbia to rescue men stranded in the wilderness. More than fifty were brought back, more dead than alive.

These stampeders reading advertisements and looking at so-called maps did not stop to think that this vast land was peopled only by a few Indians, Eskimos, and a handful of miners. They did not know that it was a huge wilderness of jagged peaks, tangled forests, and almost impassable rivers. They were unaware of the fact that no amount of gold could buy food in a land that had so few supplies and a temperature that dropped to sixty below. They did not know that it never rose above zero for months at a time, and that not even a gun could get food for them in a land where there were few animals to hunt.

Gold? The gold that was there was held by the frozen northland, under the ice and snow. It was ringed in by a wall of mountains. It was guarded by killing winds that swept down over thousands of icy miles straight from the North Pole.

12

Cheechacos!

"Inside" was the name for Alaska and the
Canadian Yukon country. "Outside" meant every
other place on earth. That's the way they talked
at the northern end of the world. And for three
years Dawson City was the hub of the universe
to prospectors, miners and cheechacos.

While the *Excelsior* and the *Portland* were
steaming south to dock at San Francisco and
Seattle with their tons of gold, Dawson was
booming. It had seven restaurants, two butcher
shops, four stores, seven gambling houses, and
two dance halls. It also boasted of its two
banks, a hospital, a telephone line and two
newspapers, *The Klondike News* and *The Nugget*.
It had two hotels. Some buildings were two
stories—with false fronts.

The swampy river bank, in Dawson, became Front Street, with Broadway and Wall Streets near by. Klondike City, just across the river from Dawson, was usually called Lousetown. In the two years since Jack Ladue had put up his saw-mill and warehouse the town had sprawled out two miles along the bank of the Yukon. By the summer of 1898 there were twelve sawmills out-side town, and they couldn't turn out enough lumber to keep up with the demand. Nails cost eight dollars a pound, and even bent and rusty second-hand nails brought almost that price.

From 1897 through 1898 Dawson City was the largest frontier town on the continent. All of Dawson was dusty with gold. Every miner with a claim had his moosehide bag with a drawstring at the top. From this poke, gold dust was weighed out to pay for everything. The miner poured out the gleaming dust for groceries, tools, drinks, clothing, and tickets to the shows. Pure gold dust was worth sixteen dollars per ounce. Gold "salted" with black sand brought eleven dollars per ounce.

So much gold dust was dropped carelessly from miners' pokes that a man who swept out a saloon made a good profit every week panning gold dust from the sawdust. Waiters kept their fingers sticky in the hope of catching gold dust. Bartenders grew long fingernails in order to pick up a little extra "dust." Every night they "panned" their fingers. Gold dust could be

97

collected from the dirt of the streets, and also from the cracks in the plank sidewalks. Nuggets weren't lying around on the ground, as the stories had claimed. But anybody could see them every day. Men wore nugget watch-chain orna-ments. Some even had them sewed on their coats as buttons. Dance-hall belles wore chains of large golden nuggets as necklaces and bracelets.

A hungry stampeder could look through a store window and see gold lying on the counter. It could be seen in boxes in the banks. Paper money was brought in after a while and began to circulate in place of some of the gold. But before long people became wary of taking it, for all kinds came in, including worthless Confederate money. It cost five dollars in gold to cash a check. Checks of all kinds were cashed. Some, scratched out on pieces of tree bark with a knife, came in from the mines. They were hon-ored, too, if the sourdoughs were known to have a good claim.

Prices were so high that they made newcomers gasp. A Dawson restaurant charged one dollar for a bowl of soup, a dollar twenty-five cents for a dish of mush and milk, and two dollars for a plate of canned tomatoes. At that time such food cost only a few cents in an eating place in the United States. The difference in price was bad enough. There was another factor that added to the high cost of living and that was the climate. For in the brisk air of the North appetites were as big as all outdoors. People joked about "the Yukon appetite." Nobody seemed to get enough to eat. *The Klondike News* published a poem about it:

> If you're going to the Yukon I'll tell you what to do,
> Be sure you take a ton of grub, or better yet, take two,
> For you'll find that you'll be hungry both morning,
>   noon and night,
> And you'll soon have what the people call a Yukon
>   appetite.

In May the ice began to break in the Yukon at Dawson City. It cracked and groaned and split with a recurring roar. People ran out to cheer and shout. Summer, with wild flowers, green trees, and a heat that could soar to a hundred degrees in the shade, would soon wipe out memories of frosted noses and bitter winds. Yet this spring thaw was unlike any other. And the Indians, moving hastily back from the river at their camp at Moosehide Creek, shook their heads. They muttered that they had not seen ice piling up like this for twenty years. Inspector Constantine went to Dawson from Fortymile at once.

Then the ice jam in the river broke, and murky water carrying big cakes of ice poured into the streets of Dawson. Soon there was a flood that rose until the people of Dawson had to move out and take to the hills. After a few days they sloshed back. They were mopping out their shacks, tents, and cabins when they heard a shout at the river:

"Cheechacos! Cheechacos! Here come the tenderfeet."

Dodging ice cakes and shouting wildly at sight of Dawson, the cheechacos came swinging in. They manned canoes, rafts and boats of every description. Faster and faster they came down the river. Dawson miners raced along the shore, jumping among cast-up pieces of river ice, yelling greetings. The new Commissioner of the Yukon, J. M. Walsh, stepped out of a canoe. He warned the town that this was only the first group. The big flood of greenhorns was yet to come.

Then, as the last cake of ice floated down the current, more than three thousand newcomers came piling into Dawson. This was an armada, filled with cheering men and a few hardy women. They were yelling, singing, beside themselves with joy at their arrival at last in the gold fields. The whole river was filled with craft. After a while the shore line was crowded and boats had to tie up to each other. Men jumped from boat to boat to reach shore. The ceaseless stream of vessels was dumping so many men into Dawson that they jammed the lodging houses and hotels. Then came a shout:

"Steamboat-a-coming!"

This would be the *Weare* or the *Bella*, everybody thought. Those were the only two boats of any size to come upriver. To everyone's surprise, it turned out to be the small *May West*.

Then, from upriver, a tiny steamboat came puffing down to Dawson. This was the one packed over Chilkoot Pass in pieces on the backs of Mr. and Mrs. Goddard. It was called the *Bellingham*, and it was only eight feet wide and thirty-five feet long. But it was the first to come downriver instead of up the Yukon.

Each new day brought some new excitement, such as the arrival of a cow to provide the first fresh milk in Dawson. A man named Miller brought her down from over the pass and then on a river scow. He sold her milk for more than twenty dollars a gallon. The cow was followed by a team of nanny goats pulling a sled loaded with a case of canned meats. The owner was able to sell not only the meat but the goats' milk also. And here came the kittens and cats, floating down on a raft. They were all sold to lonesome miners for pets. Some sourdoughs paid as much as two ounces of gold for a kitten.

A load of high rubber boots arrived and went for fifteen dollars a pair. The first crate of eggs sold as fast as the owner could hand them out. He received fourteen dollars a dozen for them. One man unloaded from his homemade boat a crate of live chickens. The crowd that gathered to watch the first egg laid in Dawson City was so big that Mounties had to keep order. Bets were laid on its arrival time. When the egg was held up by the proud owner of the hen it brought five dollars from the highest bidder.

Dawson City, spilling over into Lousetown, was a moving mass of men all day and night. They milled about in the light evenings of summer. This, they thought, was the end of the rainbow. But it would not be for most of these cheechacos. The first sourdoughs who had staked out the early claims mined fortunes in gold dust and nuggets. But the stampeders who came during this summer of 1898 found themselves paying out their money faster than they had ever imagined.

Some of them had the sense to buy a steamboat passage right away on the *Weare* or the *Bella*. They got away downriver and then took a sea-going ship for home.

Dawson was a city of restless men wandering about, unable to decide what to do. The place was filled with sound by day and by night. Sawmills buzzed. Now and then the high, shrill whistle of an arriving steamboat set everybody in town running to the river front. Men shouted, sang, and whooped it up in the saloons. Horses neighed, donkeys brayed, from dance halls came tunes played on tinny pianos. And always there was the long-drawn howling from the malamute and husky dogs tugging at their harnesses or chains.

The crowds that jammed Dawson wore every kind and description of clothing. Miners flung open their mackinaw blanket coats, parkas and sweaters as they sweated in the heat of summer. Gamblers were dandies in black broadcloth, ruffled shirts and string ties. Dance-hall girls, with plumes nodding on their big hats, paraded about in satin dresses, holding their trains up in the muddy streets. Indians wearing fringed shirts and trousers made of moose or caribou skins walked gravely to and fro. A Siwash chief, with four squaws and dog team, passed through the town on his way to the salmon rivers.

The sourdoughs, the Indians, the businessmen, and the gamblers went about the routine of their daily lives. But the new arrivals looked around them, expecting to find golden nuggets the size of goose eggs lying on the ground. And they saw nothing there but mud and stones. Some of them got out pans, picks and shovels, and went to the creeks and the hills to prospect.

But many of the newcomers seemed without interest in mining, now that they had arrived in the Klondike. They stood about on the rattling plank sidewalks, talking or trying to find old friends in the mob. When two men made contact, they sat on the edge of the sidewalk, if they could find room. Or they went down to the river-front, or sat on a keg or box somewhere and talked aimlessly. Sometimes they stood about staring at the "Great Men" of the gold fields. And one would say:

"Look. That's Pat Galvin! He's a millionaire! He's rolling in gold dust!"

"Yep," the other took it up. "They say he's cornered the waterfront too. Bought a hundred thousand dollars' worth of property in Dawson. He's putting up stores and a trading post as fast as he can get lumber and men to work on them. Made his pile on Bonanza." They stared enviously at Galvin, and edged closer.

Galvin, a former town marshall from Montana, had been one of the miners hurrying up the Yukon from Circle City at the first rumor of the strike on the Klondike. He stood out in any group, his thin figure dressed entirely in black. Wherever he went, he was followed about by a crowd of hangers-on. He kept his pockets filled with nuggets and tossed them to his followers as the whim moved him.

Two other stampeders stood talking on a wharf:

"Did you hear how Pat Galvin got a steamboat and lost it? Well, it was this way. John Irving built a big stern-wheeler and launched it down-river in grand style. It was fancy, all right. It had a big golden eagle on its pilot house. Brightest thing ever went up and down the river. But when he took on wood, that fool Irving would never move up easy-like to a landing, like other steamboat captains. No, not Irving! He charged up to each landing dock like a horse into battle—whistle open, engines stoked to the top, crew scared out of their whiskers. Well, he did it once too often. The ship crashed full on. Pat Galvin bought her and put her in for repairs.

"When she was all fixed up Pat came on board and gave every member of the crew a twenty-dollar gold piece. Then on the way to Dawson a boiler exploded. That was the end of Pat's new steamboat. Before she could be got going again she ran aground, and was frozen into the ice."

"What happened to the crew?"

"Pat bought a dog team and mushed into Dawson. The crew tried to mutiny, but all they could do was walk away."

Everybody on Front Street stared at a big man who was strolling along the sidewalk.

"Who is that?"

"Don't you know *him*?" The other cheechaco was amazed at such ignorance. "That's Big Alex

McDonald. He's called the King of the Klon-dike."

"He must have dug out a lot of gold from those creeks."

"No, he didn't dig anything. He was smart enough to stake his claims early. Then he rented them out on what they call a 'lay' to others who do the hard work. Big Alex has so many claims and gets such a lot of percentages that he is richer than anybody else. No siree! He never digs. He just uses the old brain-power. They say he buys so much property here in Dawson as well as in the mines that bets are being laid all over town as to whether by summer Big Alex will be too rich to know how much he has, or busted. Some think one. Some think the other. Me, I think he'll be richer than the King of Siam. Why? He's a canny Scotchman, that's why."

Others agreed with him. So many other claims were divided up and "lays" let out on them that nobody could tell any more who owned what out in the mines. But the thousands of cheechacos knew that newcomers, for the most part, owned nothing. They could find nothing, and soon were selling everything that they had brought with them just to buy grub.

13

Big times in Dawson

"For luck! I'll never need small change again."

The prim-looking woman in a black skirt and white shirtwaist stepping ashore from a raft in Dawson in the late autumn of 1897 had tossed a twenty-five-cent coin into the Yukon. She had drawn her coat tightly about her shoulders, for it was just before freeze-up on the river, and the wind was very cold. Then she directed the two Indians who were her paid helpers to unload her boxes of hot-water bottles and bolts of cloth. She went ahead to find a place to live, and a storage place for her goods.

Belinda Mulroney was a businesslike woman. First she built just a simple booth where she sold her bottles and cloth. They went fast, and she soon had a purse full of ready money. She put it into building log cabins in Dawson. These sold as rapidly as she could finish them. Then she bought a mule named Gerry the Bum, and hauled lumber to the mines. In the diggings, at a place called Grand Forks where two creeks came together, Belinda built a hotel. As mining claims came on the market she bought up the most promising. She also sold eggs at a dollar each. The eggs were somewhat old by the time they got to Grand Forks, but miners weren't particular. Belinda's inn was popular. So was Belinda, although she looked so starchy in her high, white collars. She permitted no rude behavior in her hotel and the sourdoughs stood in awe of her.

By the time the cheechaco fleet reached Dawson in the summer of 1898 Belinda Mulroney had built the best hotel in Dawson. She wanted it finished without delay, so she went to Skagway to get the furnishings she had ordered from the States. She would have to take everything up over the pass, and downriver. When she arrived in Skagway she found that her goods had just been dumped beside the trail. Her packers had accepted a higher fee for doing work on another shipment.

Belinda went into town and picked up a tough new crew of packers. Then she took them to where her goods lay scattered about and the pack-mules were already being loaded with the rival shipment. In no time, Belinda had a free-for-all going. Belinda's men won. They removed the other goods from the mules, loaded her supplies on, and took the cargo over White Pass. At the lake, Belinda directed the making of fifteen scows to carry her brass beds, cut-glass chandeliers, fine linen and silver safely down to Dawson. And while her men were building the scows, she kept them fed by bringing in moose-meat and salmon, for Belinda was an expert hunter and fisherwoman. When it opened, her Fairview Hotel had walls made of canvas but it was furnished in the finest style north of Seattle.

Dawson had several other independent women who could take care of themselves. There was Mrs. Wills, from Circle City, and there was Mrs. Adams. Mrs. Adams was a dressmaker who made enough money in Dawson to keep her for the rest of her life.

But most of the women who came to Dawson were singers and dance-hall girls. In the town's theatres and dance halls, miners clapped, stamped booted feet on the floor, and flung gold all over

the stage. A dance-hall girl who had a diamond fastened in her front teeth was called Diamond-tooth Gertie.

One of the first arrivals from Circle in the early days of the rush was Gussie Lamore. Gussie adored eating eggs. Eggs were often impossible to get, and when they came in they were usually pretty ripe in flavor. But that didn't bother Gussie. She just liked eggs. And a miner of small stature and large income named Swiftwater Bill Gates liked Gussie even better than Gussie liked eggs. One day he saw Gussie dining with a gambler, who was treating her to a plate of fried eggs. Overcome with jealousy, Swiftwater immediately bought every egg in town, paying for them with a coffee can full of gold dust. He gathered up half a crate of eggs. Then he took them to the middle of Front Street and, as the miners roared and cheered, broke every egg. The dogs of the town fought over them and swallowed the eggs, shells and all. From that time on, Swiftwater was also known as the Knight of the Golden Omelet.

Dawson miners rubbed shoulders with gamblers, clerks, saloon keepers, professors and writers. One day a thin gray-bearded man wearing a reindeer-skin parka pushed through the crowds, asking a miner for a meal. He was Joaquin Miller, a well-known writer from California who was often called "The Poet of the Sierras." Like many others, Miller had believed that Dawson was an easy place to live in, and that gold was lying around for the picking. So he had come in with the first crowd in the fall of 1897, as had Belinda Mulroney. But unlike the practical, hard-headed Belinda, Miller had come without food or much money, and without goods to sell. That winter he came down with scurvy. He tried to leave after freeze-up with the aid of Indian guides, but he didn't get very far. Miller came back to Dawson with his cheeks frozen, one ear gone, and snow-blind.

The gamblers and showmen did a big business in Dawson. The Mizner brothers had fingers in all sorts of schemes. Wilson, who later became a noted playwright and the owner of the Holly-wood Brown Derby restaurant, played and sang ragtime tunes. His brother Addison was later to be the famous architect of the Florida real-estate boom of the 1920s.

Others of those young men passing through the jammed Dawson streets were to become well known later. A Greek named Alexander Pantages, who owned the Orpheum Theater in Dawson, went back to California to start the Pantages theater chain. There was Sid Grauman, who was later to open the Chinese Theatre in Hollywood and to immortalize the footprints of movie stars in the cement in front of it.

When the Spanish-American War broke out, miners were frantic for news. Sid Grauman got hold of the entire shipment of newspapers telling all about it. He thought that he had made a shrewd deal when he sold Wilson Mizner the first copy for fifty dollars on the understanding that no other papers would be sold for an hour. But an hour later the price of papers had dropped to next to nothing, because Wilson had gone around charging the crowds a fee to hear him read the newspaper aloud.

Mixing with the crowds on Front Street, anybody could identify famous gunmen from the Southwest—or even Calamity Jane! There were gamblers like Tex Rickard, one of the first arrivals from Circle City. He had bought a half interest in a rich gold claim on Bonanza Creek, and began to promote prize fights in Dawson. When the gold rush ended he went to New York to become promotor of Madison Square Garden.

As the miners jostled each other in the streets, an old man called Uncle Andy ran about on nimble legs selling the local newspaper, *The Nugget*. He was sixty-five years old.

Miners just in from the diggings stood on the fringe of the crowd around a tent where piano music and the high voices of the Oatley Sisters made them feel sad. Most of them didn't have enough gold in their pokes to pay twenty dollars for a dance with one of the fabulous sisters. But they stood and listened as voices came to them from a distance trilling, "I'm Only a Bird in a Gilded Cage," or "The Daring Young Man on the Flying Trapeze." When the girls sang one of

112

the pathetic "Nellie" songs the other miners, reminded suddenly of home and family, came close to weeping.

They moved along in the streets, where booths sold everything from jewelry to furs, gold scales, picks and pans, boots and hats, satin dresses and false teeth. There were fortune tellers and troupes of acrobats, performing bears, and a man who swallowed a flaming sword over and over again.

But there was no shooting. This was Canadian territory, and the troopers of the Royal Canadian Mounted Police ran the town. First it was Inspector Constantine, who had moved to Dawson from Fortymile, who kept law and order. Then it was Superintendent Steele, coming in with the vast fleet of cheechacos down the Yukon. There was no Boot Hill here, as in the wild towns of the West, where both gunmen and their victims were buried as they were shot down.

Under the kindly but unbending law of the Mounties the diggings on the Klondike River, on Bonanza Creek, and all of the little streams called "pups," were orderly and quiet. Strangers had to surrender their guns as soon as they came into the territory.

14

The diggings

The diggings on Bonanza and Eldorado creeks were a strange world. Deep snow lay on the hills and valleys. In winter the night was dark, and the day was like a dim twilight. A swirling white fog often settled down on the gold creeks. Once there, it picked up the black smoke of the diggings, where miners kept glowing fires going around the clock. They fired the ground to soften the frozen earth, and then they dug.

Beside the mine holes, mounds of dirt and gravel rose slowly higher as men worked on in the sub-zero cold. In the distance a lone wolf put back his head and howled. Yet he could scarcely be heard for the loud creaking of the windlasses as dirt came up in buckets from the shafts.

When the men returned to their tiny cabins, where the Yukon stove in the center made a circle of warmth, a candle burning on the table was the only light. Dinner was always the same— beans, bacon and sourdough bread. Then the miners flung themselves down to sleep for a few hours. The lucky ones took time to gloat over the day's good fortune. But most of the miners had little knowledge of how much they were getting. The big mounds of earth hauled up from the underground depths had to wait until spring for what was called "the clean-up."

Every now and then during the winter a rumor would begin to circulate. In that vast land, existence itself was precarious. Travel was difficult, yet rumors spread with unbelievable speed. It was like a mysterious secret telegraph system. On a trip out for supplies one bearded miner talked confidentially to another at a bar.

"Don't tell a soul," he said, "there's a big strike over on Swede Creek."

Men listened silently, whispered, and slipped out. This was February, and the wind came like flowing ice out of the Arctic.

In no time at all there was a stampede of nearly three hundred men up Swede Creek. Dog teams floundered along in deep snow that had been unmarked until then by any track. Some men were frozen to death on that stampede. Nobody found gold. Yet the next time that a rumor started with a whisper on the street, "Gold

on the mountain," there was a wild rush out of town! Another rumor, "Gold on an island," started another stampede! So did this one, "Gold on a pup creek off the Klondike!" Men arrived there by the hundreds, only to return to Dawson in a few days, shaking their heads in disappointment.

It was a fever in the blood, a mirage in the mind! Gold! Gold! Gold!

Old sourdoughs claimed to know just the kind of place where a strike could be made. This would be in or near a creek bottom, of course. Gold was so heavy that it had to go down. They laughed and hooted at a few silly cheechacos who ranged the hills above the creeks and started

digging and panning. These hillsides were called "benches" by the miners.

On a warm day in 1897 a newcomer named Kresge, and his partner, Peterson, wandered around Bonanza Creek. They climbed the hillside above the stream, and noticed that white gravel ran there like a streak of fat in a side of bacon. They went to work on this, for they thought that here an old stream must have run thousands of years ago. And they said nothing about it, even when they found a big nugget in a shovelful of dirt.

Kresge and Peterson made a rocker, and dumped dirt into it. Then they poured in water and rocked the cradle until the dirt ran off, leaving the heavier gold. They still said nothing, but in two weeks they had found several thousand dollars' worth of gold in that rocker. Big Skookum Gulch below them had miners working on claims, but these were sourdoughs who shrugged and laughed, not believing that cheechacos would ever find gold on one of those hillside "benches." Then claims were taken out on Gold Hill by Lancaster, a man from California, who knew that gold often ran in streaks on hillsides. Lancaster's small claim was rich enough to yield more than two hundred thousand dollars' worth of gold.

Two other men, O. B. Millet and Caribou Billy Dietering, both staked bench claims on hillsides and found plenty of gold. Caribou Billy found his gold on the very top of French Hill. Millet became so ill with scurvy, a disease caused by lack of vitamin C, that he had to give up when he had taken out only about twenty thousand dollars' worth of gold. He sold the claim for sixty thousand, and the new owner made half a million dollars on it.

These lucky ones were early comers to the Klondike. They all arrived in the spring and summer of 1897. None of the men and women who came in the big stampede during the following summer found claims really worth working. Gold was there in a few creeks and hills, and in an extremely rich quantity, but the total gold area was not large. This harsh fact was not learned by the thousands who came painfully into the gold country until they were already there.

In learning it they cut down trees by the thousands to build cabins and rockers and sluice boxes. Over innumerable hills and creek banks, where wild flowers had rioted and evergreens had pointed to the sky, there was soon nothing left but holes and heaps of earth. In places, small bunches of cabins leaned close together; elsewhere they were scattered at remote distances over the hills and valleys. They stood in a jumble of makeshift engines and pumps. Windlasses rested, gaunt and shaky, on their frames near mine holes.

Miners, tired and lonesome, tramped into Dawson, or into small camp towns where they could find some amusement. Perhaps there would be a squaw to dance with? The squaw dance was one of the strangest customs in all the regions of the north.

From a nearby Indian camp the squaws slipped silently into town. They headed for a log cabin, where a fiddler was tuning up his fiddle. In the light of smoky lanterns or a few candles stuck in bottles, the Indian women removed their babies from their backs and laid them down in their cradleboards on benches against the walls. Then the squaws would begin to dance silently, in a peculiar kind of waltz. Bearded miners came in quietly, saying not a word, grabbed the squaws and danced round with them. The only sounds were made by the scraping fiddles and hobnailed boots and moccasins sliding back and forth on the floor. After several hours the squaws picked up their babies and disappeared. The miners went back to their lonely cabins.

A strange land, this north! The odd squaw dance was but one way in which the primitive customs of Indians and Eskimos were mixed with the rough ways of the miner. Yet in the towns there were reading societies and Shakespeare clubs; books were coming into libraries, and men on street corners argued over politics, philosophy and religion.

People were not always what they appeared to be in Dawson, Fortymile, or even in the tiny camp of Grand Forks, which was made up of one hotel, one saloon and a trading post. A waiter was likely to be a college professor. A bartender might be a doctor. And although a miner might live through the winter on moose-meat, sourdough bread, bacon and beans, fifty miles away hotels sold imported English plum pudding, caviar from Russia, and fresh fruit or ice cream.

In Dawson, the latest Paris gowns could be bought in a shop for a poke of gold dust. Yet in Fortymile the only broom was an equally valuable object. And when a miner got the scurvy in his lonely cabin he would have given all of the gold in his mine for a fresh tomato.

15

They came to help

"Take him to the hospital. Find Father Judge!" bystanders urged.

The miner was so ill with scurvy that his teeth had fallen out, he was too weak to talk, and he could hardly walk. He stumbled into the trading post at Grand Forks, fell on the floor, and was unable to get up. A mail carrier, bundled to the ears in his parka hood, was just starting out for Dawson over the frozen river. He took the miner along, and delivered him to St. Mary's Hospital.

This was in the spring of 1898, and there was a horde of sufferers from scurvy already in the hospital. The miner had to be put on a pad on the floor, where there was scarcely enough space left for one more patient. Father Judge came to examine him, noting the symptoms he had seen so many times before. Then he ordered a diet of minced moosemeat stewed into soup, canned tomatoes, and a tea made of spruce bark. The Indians had always known that spruce tea was a sure cure for spring scurvy. But these bearded miners, their thoughts only on gold, never listened to Indians.

Father Judge was a Jesuit missionary in Circle City when the news of the strike on Rabbit Creek emptied the town. He joined the men moving upriver. As soon as he set foot on the swampy ground of the new town already springing up with tents he made plans for a hospital. Father Judge had come to Alaska from Baltimore, Maryland, some ten or more years before. He was so thin that he looked as if a wisp of a breeze could blow him straight to the North Pole. Yet he worked day and night, a strange figure in his long black robe. In order to save the strength of the only dog that he owned, he put himself in harness beside it to pull his sled load of medicines.

The priest knew that a wave of illness—typhoid, malaria, pneumonia, bronchitis, as well as scurvy —might sweep over the new gold camp at any moment. He would do what he could for the miners.

Father Judge was stronger than he looked. He got out his tools and went to work himself on his church and hospital. He seemed to do part of every job—digging, chopping, sawing, nailing, even cooking. Then he spent his nights working on his plans by the light of a candle. He even made the rough benches, beds and other furniture. And at the end of a summer day, in the light of the Arctic night, he wandered up the hills to gather moss for mattresses, or herbs for medicinal brews.

When the church was finished, it was destroyed by a disastrous fire that in a few minutes reduced months of hard labor to a pile of smoking ashes. Father Judge immediately made plans to rebuild it. Big Alex McDonald, a Scottish Catholic, gave a large sum to help. He was joined by miners of every faith, Protestant and Catholic, Jewish and Mormon. Everybody in town wanted to help. They took up collections, and piled up gold dust and nuggets. The huskier miners pitched in with hammer and saw to complete the work on the hospital building.

The slight man with bony face and gold spectacles striding along the street in his worn black robe was a familiar sight in Dawson. He was called "the Saint of Dawson." He lived in a bare room that was also his office, and was given to sleeping on the floor, or anywhere that he could find a spot. The town felt that it should show appreciation for the unselfish help of this little priest. So miners and gamblers, housewives and dance-hall girls, got together to put on a minstrel show to raise money for the hospital. Father Judge protested that a minstrel show was not in keeping with his life. They paid no attention, and he was even persuaded to attend.

The big moment came when the priest was presented with a warm and handsome winter outfit, complete from sealskin coat to cap.

He protested. The donors wouldn't take no for an answer. He was carried up on the stage, and the warm clothing was put on him. He thanked everybody, and told them that he was not allowed to accept gifts or wear clothing of that kind. The audience only cheered and stamped. He returned to his hospital, pleased and grateful. But he still went about in his black robe in the cold of winter as well as the heat of summer.

Just after Christmas, when the weather was fifty below zero, Father Judge came down with pneumonia. Miners stood in little knots on the

streets, their faces turning now and then toward the small log hospital under the scarred hill behind the town.

Gambling rooms, dance halls and stores closed their doors. Some Indians came silently into town, and stood about waiting. When word spread that Father Judge had died the whole town was draped in black. The entire population—Protestants, Catholics, those of other faiths—all went to the funeral. It took crews of hard-working men two and a half days to dig a grave in the frozen earth.

Meanwhile another hospital was being built in Dawson. This was called the Good Samaritan. It was a non-sectarian hospital, designed to take care of the large number who could not find room in St. Mary's. Dawson was bursting with people, and thousands more would be coming with the spring thaw on the Yukon.

There were three other churches in Dawson— one for Presbyterians, another for Episcopalians, and one for Methodists. There were also Salvation Army units—singing, beating drums and tambourines—holding their meetings on the streets.

Like Father Judge, Protestant ministers and bishops had come to the Yukon and Alaska long before this stampede. They worked with the miners as well as with the Indians and Eskimos in their lonely villages among the snows. Years before gold was found on the Klondike, Bishop Bompas of the Church of England had come to

Fortymile. He was alarmed by what he saw. He wrote to Ottawa that Indians were being sold whiskey by miners—a disastrous thing! He wrote also that the shootings in Fortymile which, although technically in Canadian territory, was filled with Americans, must be stopped. It was his plea that brought Superintendent Constantine and his detachment of Mounted Police to Fortymile with immediate results. The camp where lawless men shot and knifed each other in saloons and on muddy streets changed with startling rapidity. The outlaws crossed back to Alaskan territory.

Bishop Bompas had taken the place of an earlier missionary who had gone insane because of the cruel and senseless jokes of the outlaws and miners in Fortymile. The jokers soon found that Bompas was not easily scared. He was a huge man, with a long nose, stern eyes, and a beard. He was a graduate of Cambridge University, and a scholar of Greek, Latin and Hebrew. Like Father Judge, he learned to fold up in a corner of a boat, or to stretch out on a floor or a bench when he got the chance to sleep. He led a simple, hardy life, invariably making his own sourdough bread, and had no eating utensils except a knife, a tin cup, and a plate.

Wherever Bishop Bompas traveled—whether it was to an Eskimo or Indian village—he was always welcome. Once he gave his trousers to a sick Indian, and went home in his red flannel underwear. The Bishop lived this rough and strenuous life alone for five years, and then his English wife came to the North to join him. She arrived in 1892, bringing with her a small parlor organ as well as a shelf of books, many of them written in Italian. She had grown up in Italy, with a doctor's family.

After a time the Bishop's wife began to accompany her husband on long treks to lonely Eskimo camps. She grew used to riding in a dog sled bundled in furs. She learned to eat the rancid meat of seal and whale with the Bishop's parishioners. She helped doctor small Indian children who were ill with eye disease or scurvy.

In August, 1897, a vigorous Presbyterian missionary named Hall Young arrived in Alaska. He brought with him the Reverend George A. McEwen. They landed at Dyea, joined the first early flood of stampeders, and began the high climb over the Chilkoot Pass. Young and McEwen made the trip down the Yukon just before freeze-up, reaching Dawson early in October.

Mr. Young searched for a building suitable for a church, and could find nothing but a large log cabin owned by a saloonkeeper. Here he announced services immediately, working day and night to get the church ready. He used blocks of wood and hand-hewn logs for seats, and borrowed a miner's copper blower for a collection plate.

When the Presbyterian church had been in use for only a month fire broke out, and it suffered

the same fate as the chapel built by the Catholic priest. The loss amounted to more than a thousand dollars. Young and McEwen began at once to look for another place to hold services. They rented the Pioneer Hall, and soon had a congregation of fifty people. When a spring flood washed into Pioneer Hall, the Presbyterians joined the Episcopalians for a while.

So Dawson had all sorts of people, and all sorts of ways. It was filled with contrast. On Saturday nights there was the noise of singing, dancing and gambling—but no shooting. On Sunday there was no sound except quiet voices, the howling of huskies and malamute dogs, and the sound of hymn-singing from the churches.

16

Dogs of the gold rush

Dawson was a city of dogs, and the dominant sound of the gold rush was the yapping, snapping, barking, howling of the dogs. In this town in the middle of the gold country there was one dog to every three or four persons. In that first winter of the stampede, before the great rush of cheechacos, the only animals in Dawson were dogs—except for a few horses and one mule. There wasn't a cat, or a cow, or a goat, or a sheep, or even a chicken! There were at least fifteen hundred dogs.

During the day dogs were tied up along the main streets, ready to mush out at a moment's notice. They waited while the dog driver went into a restaurant for a cup of beef soup. With a trip in the intense winter cold ahead of him, no

dog driver would drink anything alcoholic. He knew that if he took a drink of whiskey the cold would kill him faster. At night there were dogs in back of most of the cabins, curled into the snow in furry balls, woolly tails wrapped around noses, sleeping as happily as a boy would in bed.

Some were dogs from Outside—St. Bernards or Newfoundlands. A few collies and a lot of mixed breeds came in with the first cheechacos in late May and June of 1898. More came in all through that summer. But in the winter, before they came, the Inside dogs outnumbered the Outside dogs many times over.

The few Outside dogs had to be able to fight like wolves to survive. They had to face malamutes, huskies, and Siwash Indian dogs—all with wolf blood in them.

Miners had to step over dogs lying all over the wooden sidewalks. They had to find their way between dogs in the frozen dirty snow of the street. A frequent diversion was a dog fight. Men standing about, just in from lonely mining shacks, stepped over to watch, making bets on the winner.

"Look at that yaller dog go!" a miner shouted one day. "He'll take on a malamute any day in the morning."

The yellow dog, a big mixed breed with long matted hair, was a real fighter. He would stand up to any of the gray or black huskies or malamutes, fierce as they were. He made a white Eskimo dog turn tail and run, howling. But despite all the snarling and fighting, as a rule not much blood was drawn in these dog battles. The big dogs of the North had fur so thick and matted that it served not only as protection from the cold but also kept a fighting enemy's teeth from reaching the skin.

Men were yelling, the street was crowded, and about thirty dogs, still fighting among themselves, had drawn away to leave the field to the yellow animal. Three black huskies advanced together on the yellow dog. They looked like snarling bears.

"Not a fair scrap," protested a bystander. "Grab 'em!"

Four dog drivers in the crowd dashed into the battleground, seized the huskies and held on. The snarling quieted down. The crowd melted away, bets forgotten. Soon the dogs all lay down in the street again and went to sleep, the yellow one not far from his three black enemies. They had nothing against each other. It was all part of a day's activities.

Sometimes it seemed as if the dogs ran Dawson. They were everywhere. They wandered into houses, saloons, restaurants and banks. Men were constantly driving them outside, swatting and shouting at them. They were not pets, these dogs of the North.

The outstanding pet of Dawson was a mule named Gerry. He belonged to Belinda Mulroney, who ran the Fairview Hotel, and he had a taste for hard liquor. All day long Gerry wandered into saloon after saloon, begging drinks until he was pushed out by the miners. They knew that Belinda was fond of Gerry and wouldn't like it if they gave him drinks.

When the stampede was at its height, Dawson

was a noisy, riproaring gold-mining town. But it was different from American frontier places, because the Mounties ran it. There were only a few Mounties, but they were not disobeyed.

"Any man we can't control gets a blue ticket," they warned. "That means he's out of town by morning!" And by morning he *was* on his way.

"Get on the woodpile!" was another command that meant punishment. The gambler caught cheating at cards got six months of hard labor sawing and splitting wood. That woodpile behind the Mounties' barracks was a dreaded place. It was a huge woodpile, built for a long winter.

And when the Mounties said, "No work, no entertainment on Sunday," they meant it.

One Sunday the livelier element in town turned out for a dog-team race. The two most famous dog teams in Dawson were spoiling to prove themselves the faster. Half the miners in town bet on one team, and the rest on the other. It was early in the morning when dance-hall girls in their long skirts, fur coats and flowered hats lined up along the road outside of Dawson. With them were gamblers wearing black suits and hats, fur coats and gloves. Miners crowded in, eyes glittering with excitement.

Far down the course the fine dog teams lined up. Their expert drivers were behind the sleds, mittened hands on the gee-poles. A loud "Hurrah!" rang out.

"Mu-s-s-sh!" yelled the drivers.

"Here they come!" Everybody strained forward, almost falling into the hard-packed snow of the trail. Down the stretch the dog teams raced, neck and neck.

Suddenly two men in fur-lined parkas stepped into the trail directly in front of the onrushing dog teams. The whole crowd groaned, the sound echoing from the hill behind the town. They didn't need the glimpse of yellow-striped pants to realize that the law had taken over. The big Sunday race was over. Everybody trouped back to town, and all bets were off. The Mounted Police had said, "No racing on Sunday," and they meant it. The owners of the teams of huskies went to work on the woodpile.

The word heard most often along the trails was the command to go—"Mush!" It came from the command *"Marchons!"* (meaning "Go!") used by French-Canadian dog drivers working for the Hudson's Bay Company in the north. Americans hearing the French word *marchons* turned it into "Mush on!" Eskimos used other words of their own in commanding their teams of dogs— such as *"Owk,"* meaning "Go to the right," *"Arrah,"* for "Go to the left," or *"Halt,"* meaning "Go straight ahead."

To the Eskimo and the Indian of the North the dog is the beast of burden, as the horse and mule are to the man who lives in warmer climates. In late winter of 1898 as many as eighteen or twenty dog teams from far-flung Indian camps

134

gathered in Dawson, their sleds loaded with the season's catch. The Indians traded their furs and game, loaded up with supplies, and disappeared again to their remote camps.

The largest Indian village was Moosehide, a few miles down the Yukon from Dawson. Unlike many of the villages of the wandering Indian tribes of the Yukon Territory, this was not a temporary camp. Here the Moosehide Indians, under Chief Isaacs, lived in log cabins. Chief Isaacs was a great hunter of moose and caribou, and a great fisher of salmon. He was respected for his wisdom as well as his strength and endurance. And while most Indian dogs were of an inferior breed, closer to wolf, Chief Isaacs owned the finest teams of huskies in the Yukon.

Yet all of the huskies—malamutes and "Siwash Indian dogs," as the wild and downtrodden kind was called—had uncontrollable appetites. Any dog in the Alaska and Yukon country would eat anything. This was true even of a dog worth four or five hundred dollars. A malamute or a husky could be a good friend to his master, and guide him safely through blizzards and over icy trails that seemed impassable. Yet the same dog could be a thief. He had to be watched at all times. He would eat his leather harness if he could get at it. He would eat his master's mukluks—the sealskin boots worn by Eskimos and by dog drivers or others who had to be out in the snows. He would eat a greasy dishcloth with one snap of his powerful jaws.

Everywhere in the frozen North small log houses rested on stilts built high above the ground. These little storehouses were called by a French word, *cache*. They were as important as the cabins, stoves and firewood. Without the cache a miner would starve. Wolves, bears and dogs would take any kind of food not kept in the cache.

A husky would steal a can of meat, bite it open in a few seconds, and disappear with the contents instantly. It was said that any dog could read the label on a can at sight, and would know enough to steal meat rather than marmalade! There were stories of dogs who formed partnerships—one to distract the owner's attention, and the other to steal the stewpot full of moosemeat right off the Yukon stove. He would take the pot by the handle, race out of the cabin with it, and hide it in the snow until it was cold. Then he would be joined by his companion, and they would fight fiercely over the spoils.

Once a miner was sitting in his cabin with a lighted candle on the table. He closed his eyes for a moment, and opened them just in time to see his gray malamute sneak in by the door that he had not locked. The dog snatched the candle and swallowed it, flame and all!

As a regular thing dogs were fed dried salmon once every twenty-four hours, and always at night. For a team had to do a full day's work to earn its supper, and the dogs knew that.

"Who has the best dog team in the Klondike?" somebody might ask.

"Why, Captain Bennett, of course," would be the answer.

Captain Bennett of the Alaska Commercial Company was a friend of the Indians. In the winter of 1898 everybody was on short rations, and everybody talked about probable starvation if supplies couldn't get through before spring. The Captain heard that some Indians were already in trouble. Fifty of them from Porcupine Creek had failed to find caribou herds, and had had nothing to eat for days except one rabbit and three or four weasels.

Bennett immediately organized a relief expedition. Despite short supplies in Dawson he packed food on sleds, mustered his best drivers, and set out. When he found the starving Indians he was careful not to offend them. He told their chief that he had come to give a "potlatch," or feast. At the end of the meal the chief, who had resisted many offers to buy his team of huskies, offered to sell them to Captain Bennett. They were great gray fellows, originally from the Mackenzie River country, larger and finer than any that the Captain had even seen. Bennett paid seventeen hundred dollars for five dogs, and thought, rightly, that he had made a good bargain. He also took the Indians to Fort Yukon, where he gave them another big "potlatch."

In winter snows and across the ice there was no way to travel except by dog team. Dogs did everything. They were used to haul lumber, supplies and people. Once on Bonanza Creek a miner saw a team of dogs hauling a sled load of green-spruce lumber weighing sixteen hundred pounds. Each dog team had a leader. This dog was strong and wise and had high regard for his position. He would do his job well, without stopping. If another dog caused trouble, he would often bring him to terms and make him work, too. The leader stood for no nonsense.

In summer, dogs sometimes carried packs weighing as much as forty or fifty pounds on their backs. They rarely bit a human, but they would tear into another dog over food, for they never seemed to get enough to eat. A good dog team would haul as much as five hundred pounds on the trail, and could run twenty-five miles in six hours. Sometimes the drivers put leather boots on the dogs to protect their feet from sharp ice, but aside from that they had little care.

In 1899 a team of huskies was sold to the Canadian Development Company in Dawson to haul mail back and forth from Whitehorse, a new town that had sprung up on the upper Yukon River. The team cost the company three thousand, five hundred dollars.

During the early part of the gold rush the Mounted Police carried the mail with dog teams.

They had posts along the Yukon twenty to forty miles apart. Here they changed dogs and went right on as fast as they could travel over the snow. They brought in dog drivers from the Northwest Territory who were expert and kind. Whenever the Mounties found anyone in their territory mistreating his dogs, the man was arrested. Until 1899, when horses took over, dog teams brought in the mail over White Pass. They ran nearly a thousand miles with it, and they made an average of thirty-two miles a day.

Out of Dawson there were dog-stage lines that took one or two passengers on a regular run, and there were private passenger sleds also. The crime that brought the heaviest punishment in Dawson was dog stealing. A dog thief was held in as much contempt there as a horse thief was in the American West, and he was lucky if the Mounties got him before the miners did. He was glad to take his blue ticket and get out of town—fast.

One of the better-known inhabitants of Dawson was a prospector called the Windy Kid. He had a good fast team of dogs for which he had paid three hundred dollars. He got his nickname from talking so much about new strikes, and yet always being mysterious about them. If anybody saw the Windy Kid harnessing up his dog team late at night, the word would get about town. "New Strike! Where? Don't know yet. But I must be ready to run. The Windy Kid's harnessing up his team."

When the Kid grabbed the gee-pole and shouted "Mush," half the miners of the town were right behind. But the Kid's team was fast, and the followers were soon outdistanced. Yet the Windy Kid never did make a really good strike. He never had much gold dust in his poke, never more than enough to buy salmon for his team and beans and bacon for himself.

17

Gunfire in Skagway!

It was four days after the Fourth of July, 1898, and the town of Skagway was still trying to recover from the big celebration. Even the Governor of Alaska had come from the capital at Sitka to sit beside Mr. Jefferson Randolph Smith, better known as Soapy, on the platform where flags waved. The governor was supposed to have been the honored guest, but everybody had stared at Soapy, for by now he was called the "Uncrowned King of Skagway."

Now, wearing a look of satisfaction, Soapy Smith walked down Broadway. He was a slender man, dressed in black broadcloth, with a heavy gold chain dangling across his vest. He tipped his wide-brimmed gray hat to a lady who, pleased to be noticed, smiled prettily. As he passed a small

boy the "King of Skagway" leaned over to pat
the child on the head. With his other hand he
tossed him a five-dollar gold piece. The boy
scrambled around for it in the dusty street,
shouting with glee.

People spoke respectfully. "Morning, Mr.
Smith. Howdy, Mr. Smith. How are you, Jeff?"

Nobody dared call him "Soapy" to his face
now. The days when Smith had tricked people
out of money by selling bars of soap were over.
He had come a long way from the camps of
Colorado. But he was still the same man who
had invented the phrase, "sure-thing game."

"I'm not the usual gambler," he said. "When
I stake my money it's a sure thing I'll win."

A bent and bearded miner, his clothing dirty
from the long trip up the Yukon and over White
Pass, came plodding into Skagway. He had a
pack on his back. The right-hand pocket of his
coat bulged with the special kind of bulge that
signified a poke of gold dust inside. He stopped
on the sidewalk, let others push past him, shoved
his rusty hat back on his head, and stared at
Jeff Soapy Smith.

"Who's that?" he asked of nobody in particular.

"Why, ain't you the greenhorn," replied a boy,
"Soapy himself, that is. Good morning, Mr.
Smith. How are you today?"

Mr. Smith disappeared into his oyster parlor,
where oysters were sold in the restaurant in

front, and in the back rooms naive miners were swindled of their gold. In his office Jeff Smith leaned back in his chair and spoke to two of his men—the "Reverend" Bowers, who looked like a preacher, and Old Man Tripp, the exact image of an ignorant stampeder from "Outside."

"Bowers, I passed a sourdough just now," Smith said. "He's right off the trail, and has a good poke, I'll bet. You and Tripp go after him." Bowers nodded, for his keen eye had also spotted the miner. He and Tripp went out to do their master's bidding. Smith swiveled his chair around and spoke to his aide. "Did you send some money to the widow of that man I shot? And how about a contribution to the church? Don't forget it. It's the first toward a fund for their new building. If the preacher gets a fund going, we can manage a little robbery and get our contribution back—bigger than we gave."

Soapy was attending to his business of the day. He was a busy man. Half the town thought him generous, kind and most pleasant. The other half knew him better. They knew him to be cold, cruel, thieving, conniving and worse. Yet he never soiled his hands with the rough and dirty work. He just directed it, like the king he considered himself to be.

Only four months before, Soapy had had to contend with a Vigilante Committee ready to run him out of town. He had dealt with that threat. He had bribed some, threatened others, blackmailed a few and, by accusing them of the very things he did himself, brought about the end of the Vigilante Committee.

Those who really hated Soapy were the handful of tough, strong and honest frontiersmen who had wandered into Skagway. These were men who had fought Indians in the army, or who had been marshals or sheriffs in various Western frontier towns. Some had been cowpokes, and were now businessmen of Skagway. A man named Frank Reid had come there to survey the town, and had stayed on. He was the only man whom Soapy Smith feared, and Frank Reid feared nobody. But right now he was able to do nothing against the "King of Skagway."

The newly arrived miner, Stewart by name, was already in the friendly tow of the two thieves, who looked harmless and good-natured. Stewart had been on his way to the bank to deposit his poke, containing two thousand, five hundred dollars' worth of gold. Now he had decided to let these good, new friends take care of it for him in Mr. Smith's safe. He was steered into that comfortable back room, where a table invited a card game first. But Stewart suspected card games. When his new friends became insistent he turned on his worn boot heel to leave.

At that point, Old Man Tripp, looking for all the world like a Klondiker himself, grabbed the heavy poke as if he were joking, and ran out the back door. Stewart, whirled around by the other man, stumbled out through the same door and looked about him, dazed. He was in a back yard that had a high fence around it. There was no sign of the thief or the gold poke. Stewart had no way of knowing that Tripp had slipped out of the yard through a small secret door in the fence.

Stewart was a slow man. But now he was angry. He rushed out to the street, and found a deputy marshal, but got no help there. The deputy of course was in Soapy's pay. Then Stewart went to a horse packer who had brought some of his things in over the pass. The packer told his boss, who was a friend of Frank Reid. This was in the morning of July 8. By noon the Vigilante Committee was reorganizing. The good citizens of Skagway had been waiting for the chance. Now they had it.

The Vigilantes brought over a judge from Dyea, who ordered Soapy to give back the gold by four in the afternoon, or there would be trouble—real trouble. Soapy lost his temper. This he seldom did, for he was ordinarily too smooth an operator for that. But Soapy had thought that he really had things his own way when he sat on that platform beside the Governor of Alaska, and then rode at the very front of the Fourth of July parade, heading his own military company. Why, Soapy really thought that most of the men and women of Skagway liked him. How could they help it? He gave money to charity. He was the man who had put up the recruiting tent to sign up volunteers for the Spanish-American War.

146

Now he found out just how much he was liked. As he walked through town the climate had changed. Now people drew away from him. They stared, but not with envy and admiration. They were scared. So was he—for the first time!

"Better return that poke to the Klondiker," advised the "Reverend" Bowers.

"I'll kill the man who tries to make me give it back," shouted Soapy, his face swelling with rage.

He got out his pistol, and shoved it in the holster. Then he picked up his Winchester rifle, and strode out into the street. He stalked up and down for a little while. A member of his gang came running up. "There's a Vigilante meeting starting at Sperry's Warehouse," he said. "Want we should get in there and break it up?"

Soapy nodded, and set off for the warehouse himself.

As his men mingled with the crowd going in, he himself advanced directly toward the door, gun in hand. At the door stood Frank Reid. Soapy gave Reid a shove that knocked him down. Reid jumped up and ordered him away. Noting several grim-looking men with guns standing behind Reid, Soapy retreated and made for a saloon. Ordinarily Smith wasn't a drinking man, for he knew that to run his involved affairs he had to have a clear head. Now, however, he took several drinks of whiskey.

Sometime later he was out on the street again. He could see that people edged fearfully away from him. His head began to pound, and the blood rushed to it.

A gunman named Foster approached and said, "Jeff, we broke up that meeting, all right. But they're getting another one going right now."

"All right. Break that one up, too," Smith ordered.

Slim Jim Foster pushed his hat back and rubbed his chin. "How? They're meeting at the end of the long wharf, with guards at the land end."

Soapy clutched his gun with both hands, and turned away. He walked toward the wharf, though a bit unsteadily. Now he no longer looked like a kind, smiling Southern gentleman. His gold watch chain swung from side to side. His face was wild and bloated looking. As he came to the wharf people moved away from him. He was alone except for about a dozen of his men who marched behind him in a solid group, guns drawn.

At the entrance to the wharf a chain had been fastened, and Reid, with two others, was letting people through. They swung around as they saw Soapy advancing. The air crackled with excitement. Out at the far end of the long dock men were holding a meeting to argue over what to do about Soapy.

Soapy raised his rifle and fired at Frank Reid. At the same instant Reid drew his own gun but it misfired. Soapy's bullet hit him in the shoulder. As Soapy fired again so did Reid. Soapy dropped onto the boards of the dock, dead. Reid fell, too, badly wounded in two places. Someone yelled, and then the crowd surged along the wharf, pounding forward until the dock shook on its slender posts. As a couple of men lifted Frank Reid to take him to the hospital, he managed a little smile. "I got him, boys," he said.

After that the whole town of Skagway went wild. There wasn't a gambler, thief, or confidence man who was safe from hanging that night. Eleven were arrested and clapped into jail before ropes could be knotted around their necks. Several, including Old Man Tripp and the preacher-like Bowers, found refuge in the woods. They couldn't escape over White Pass because the Mounted Police on top would have been

more than happy to take them into custody. They couldn't get out on the cold waters of the inlet, for they had no boats. There was nowhere to escape. The town of Dyea would have welcomed a chance to collar them. Mosquitoes nearly ate them up, and before many hours had passed they were as hungry as Kodiak bears in springtime. Finally Tripp announced that he was going back to Skagway to get a good meal, and give himself up.

"They've got the rope ready. They'll hang us sure," one of his pals warned.

"Well, hanging's just twenty years overdue," said Old Man Tripp. "I'd rather hang than starve."

Stewart's poke of gold was found in a trunk at Soapy's place, with most of its contents intact. It was returned to Stewart. The Baptist and the Methodist ministers refused to preach the funeral sermon for Soapy. The Presbyterian minister finally agreed to do it alone. He was guarded by a Vigilante with a gun. Frank Reid lingered on for several days. An operation was tried, but it was unsuccessful. A few days later he died, and all of Skagway attended his funeral.

The burial place of Jefferson Randolph Smith, otherwise called Soapy, had a gravestone after a while, surrounded by wire to keep souvenir hunters from taking it away bit by bit. The grave of resolute and fearless Frank Reid was marked by a piece of marble. On it was cut, "He gave his life for the honor of Skagway."

18

Dawson burns!

April 20, 1899, was a cold day. Towards evening, Sam "the Moose" stepped outside his cabin for just a moment to peer at his new "thermometer." This was of the makeshift type that most people in the Klondike used. On the snow that he had scooped into a shelf and packed down hard, Sam had placed a saucer with a bit of mercury on it, and next to that a bottle of Perry Davis Pain Killer medicine, which was almost pure alcohol.

He looked hard at the mercury. "Yep, frozen." Sam "the Moose" nodded, and looked at the bottle of pain-killer. Then he whistled, shoving out the ledgelike lower lip that had given him his nickname. "Solid! Well! Must be forty-five below." He dodged hastily back inside the eight-foot-high snow tunnel leading to his cabin door and muttered, "Spring. Who would think it?"

A little way down the street in Dawson, cabins, stores, banks and the post office were glowing with candle- and lamplight. The early dusk shimmered with it, but not many people ventured out into the intense cold. The cabin housing the new fire engine was dark, for the firemen were on strike for better wages. They had let their fires go out, and the steam pumpers were cold and empty.

That night, as most of the town slept, the gauzy curtains in a room above a saloon burst into flame. In seconds the whole building was on fire. The dim streets filled with dogs, howling and yapping, men shouting and yelling, and women screaming and crying.

"Fire! Fire! Fire!"

Belinda Mulroney, capable manager of her Fairview Hotel, threw on her reindeer parka, drew on mukluks, and ran outside. She saw that already half of Front Street was ablaze, shooting flames straight up into a dark sky that was without the smallest wind. A fog made by the heat of the fire hitting the cold air above settled over Dawson.

Men were running, building fires that would melt holes through the river ice and thus enable them to get water to put out the fire. Up and down Front Street building after building was crackling and flaming. Sam "the Moose" joined the firefighters. Others lined up to watch the fire engines begin to fill hoses from the holes in the ice, and then help haul them across the street. But the hoses grew stiff and heavy as the water in them froze.

"It's going to bust. Look out!" somebody yelled.

The men dropped the hoses as the leather seams burst with a loud pop. This was followed by a groan that spread along the street like the moaning of the winter wind straight from the polar ice. There was no hope now for the town of Dawson. Flames swept higher.

"There goes the bank!" came an anguished cry.

"The bank vault . . . it's gone!" rose another.

A crowd milled around the fire, near the bank. The big vault burst open and they could plainly see a mass of nuggets, gold dust, jewelry, paper money and valuables of many kinds melting into one lump in the soggy snow.

Bill McPhee's Pioneer Saloon was blazing when he dashed inside. He came out tenderly holding a huge moosehead whose antlers branched out over him.

"He'd rather lose everything he's got than that moosehead," commented a friend. "It's been with him ever since he came to Dawson."

Belinda Mulroney fed the firefighters when they stumbled, exhausted, into her hotel lobby.

A gambler twirled his waxed moustache and shrugged, saying, "Well, easy come, easy go. It's

all in the toss of a card."

A pack of several hundred dogs, crazed by the uproar, ran across the frozen river and disappeared. Most of them returned in a state of starvation after several days, but the others joined wolf packs and never returned.

The teams of horses and dogs were put to use hauling goods out of buildings and outside of town to the frozen swamp at the foot of the mountain. It was plain enough to see that the Aurora Saloon and the building next to it were doomed.

"We'll have to blow her up," said Captain Starnes of the Mounted Police, his face grim.

He sent a dog team to a warehouse out of town for dynamite for the job. When it arrived the charge was set. As the town watched, a blast shook the frozen earth and seemed to make the very mountain quiver. The Aurora was gone, in a pile of rubble, and the fire was stopped from spreading farther on that side. The firemen, joined by hundreds of volunteers, worked all night and into the next day. At last they had the fire under control, and the town could stand back and see the destruction caused by one small candle.

A million dollars' worth of property was ruined, and Dawson had lost most of its larger buildings. The Fairview Hotel was saved, as were a few others. Yet next day, in the intense cold that still held the town tightly in its grip, there was the noise of wreckage being cleared. Hammers and saws soon sounded loudly, and lumber was coming in for rebuilding.

Sam "the Moose" stared at the place where his cabin had stood. It was a mess of ashes. He pulled his parka hood down over his face, and then he turned and wandered off, muttering, "Spring. Who would think it?"

As May brought the first thaw, miners came straggling into Dawson from their cabins on creeks and in gulches. One of them was Jack London. He had earned three thousand dollars steering boatloads of cheechacos down the White Horse Rapids. Then he had gone prospecting, but could not locate a good claim. Winter found him on the Stewart River, living in a cabin abandoned by another prospector.

He had enough money for food, and he had the books he had brought in with him. There were several other cabins near by. In the dark days and nights of that winter men gathered in London's cabin to talk and read aloud. Some were ministers, others were doctors, teachers and lawyers. They discussed everything from politics to literature. Uneducated miners who joined them argued and discussed every subject too. Here, in his snowbound cabin, Jack London heard tales told by the Malamute Kid, Burning Daylight, and other sourdoughs. There were stories related by Mounties and by dog drivers.

When spring came Jack London was ill with scurvy. His teeth were falling out, and he could just manage to get to Dawson and to the hospital. As soon as he was on his feet again he and several companions made a boat and set off down the Yukon. At St. Michaels he shipped as a sailor on a vessel. When Jack London reached San Francisco again he was no richer in gold than he had ever been. But he came back crammed with stories of the frozen North. Later they took form in his books, the best-known of which is *The Call of the Wild*, and many short stories. Jack London became the most famous writer of the Klondike and the Alaska gold rush.

By July of 1899, Dawson City was rising from

its ashes. The new buildings were better than the old. Also, there were water pipes and sanitation. Dawson became a better place in which to live. In fact, Dawson was becoming a permanent town.

Down the Yukon that summer came a man with some news. His name was Dr. Loyal Wirt, and he was on his way with two companions to the far western coast of Alaska on the Bering Sea. He had come by way of White Pass and the lakes. There he had built a boat of green lumber, and joined the cheechacos still coming into the Klondike.

In Dawson, where he landed to buy supplies before pushing off again, Dr. Wirt answered many questions.

"I'm taking charge of the camp on Bering Sea. There's a gold strike there. No, I'm not a prospector. The governor asked me to go in to try to help those people."

Dr. Wirt had no sooner left than miners began to scramble for boats. The rumor spread quickly through the diggings. Hand-panning was not paying much now. The gold still came out of the earth in the Klondike. But it came out only with the aid of machinery, not by hand. Mining companies were washing down the hillsides with hydraulic hoses, and big dredges were brought in to work through the mud of the creek bottoms.

"Strike on the beach of Bering Sea. Where is it? How should I know?" one prospector hastily told another. "It's somewhere north of St.

Michaels, I reckon. How to get there? Why, just go downriver, and then up the coast by ship. Am I going? Sure, I'm going."

The prospector was already stuffing clothing and grub into his pack. He was tying onto it his shovel, pick and pan. He was crowding into the first boat that was leaving Dawson—if he could wedge himself aboard.

That was the beginning of the end for Dawson. From that day on the town would never again be the hub of the great gold rush. There were to be no more days when a thousand newcomers hit town, and miners by the thousand climbed the hills and waded the streams of the Klondike. That was the end of the search for claims, of the driving of stakes, of the rush for the recorder's office. Now the big hydraulic hoses and the dredges would have the Klondike to themselves.

"I'm off for the new strike," was the parting shout of the old sourdough.

And now the cheechaco of last year was the sourdough of this year. It took the passing of a year—one sight of breaking ice in the Yukon, one winter of living on sourdough bread—to make a sourdough. Or, at any rate, that's what they said in Dawson.

19

The rush to Nome

Dr. Wirt and his companions swung down the Yukon current, followed by a flotilla of makeshift boats from Dawson and the other settlements along the shores. The seagoing ship that he boarded at St. Michaels was crowded to the scuppers. These stampeders were nearly all full-fledged sourdoughs by now, yet they were just as frantic as the cheechacos had been on the passes, up the Yukon, and on the long overland trails.

The captain spoke slowly, but with emphasis. "I'm glad you're going to the beach, Dr. Wirt. There isn't anybody there to take charge—no law, nothing."

Dr. Wirt leaned over the rail as the ship dropped anchor offshore, and looked long at this new land. It was so far north that the polar ice

pushed hard on the beach in winter. It was a
hundred and fifteen miles above St. Michaels, on
the Bering Sea across from Siberia. It was nothing
but a flat stretch of gray beach, with frozen
tundra behind it and farther off some low hills.
There were no trees, and no bushes. It was a
cold and empty land, the land of wandering
Eskimo tribes.

Now the shoreline was crowded. Tents made a
town, and as Dr. Wirt came in to shore he could
see that all over the beach men were digging.
These sands were rich with gold. In the center of
the tent town a few gray buildings stood out.
They were made of driftwood washed in by the
waves.

As the five hundred miners on board ship
neared shore they splashed and waded the last
few steps. Then they made for the far edges of

the crowd on the beach, and began to stake claims even before they had set up their tents. They saw that miners with rich claims were panning out the wet sand right from the edge of the sea. Each little group of men had a rocker, and while one man rocked it back and forth, others poured in water from a tin can, or even from their rubber boots. Still others were digging out sand and dumping it into the rocker with their bare hands, or with a piece of a board, if they were lucky enough to have such a thing.

Dr. Wirt stood on the beach for a while watching the excited scene. Now and then a yell of joy broke out.

"Whoopee!" A mass of miners poured toward the sound to see how much gold had come out of a pan.

Dr. Wirt moved along, and then stopped to

look at small groups of men sitting on the ground with packs of greasy cards. There were others bunched around a man who was expertly placing three walnut shells and a pea. The doctor also observed miners with dice. All of these men were losing their gold as fast as they collected it. He shook his head, and strode into the tent town. As he went he heard a man ask, "Who's that? He's not staking a claim."

One of the prospectors from the recently arrived ship answered, "That's a doctor sent up here by the Governor of Alaska. He's going to look after the sick, I reckon."

Dr. Wirt found plenty of illness in the town. Under the midnight sun, with the evening sky the color of rose, violet and yellow, there was a scent of frying flapjacks all the time. These men slept when they were worn out, and worked when they pleased. There was no regular sleeping time, for darkness did not come regularly, as they were used to. Many were lying in their tents ill with scurvy, pneumonia or dysentery. The doctor got out his medicines and went right to work. This was a hard job, for there was no hospital and he had no trained help.

The day after his arrival he found a responsible miner, and talked over the situation with him. He asked whether anybody there realized that winter was coming soon. There would be nine months of severe cold, he warned, and no contact at all with the outside world. The man looked thoughtful, and went away to discuss it with others. A new cemetery grew rapidly behind the town. The tent city was governed by the usual miners' meeting. One such meeting was held to name the camp.

The newly elected chairman stood on the bottom of an overturned boat, shouting, "This meeting is called to name the town." He pointed to the ice pack now pushing down against the sands. "How about Iceberg City?"

"No. How about Anvil City?" A sourdough pointed to the hill behind the camp. A rock on top of it was shaped like a blacksmith's anvil.

So the camp became known as Anvil City. Later its name was changed to Nome.

Dr. Wirt had been there only three days when the miner to whom he had talked came to him with a big poke filled with gold. It had been collected from the people of the town, who realized now that a hospital, doctors and nurses were needed at once. There was also a food problem. Could Dr. Wirt go out with this gold, and bring back everything needed? The poke had six thousand dollars' worth of gold in it.

Dr. Wirt took it, and went aboard the next ship sailing for Seattle. There he spent ten days buying supplies and enlisting doctors and nurses. He also bought lumber. He chartered an old whaling vessel, loaded it with his new expedition, and with his wife returned to Nome. The ship dropped anchor off the beach with only a few days to spare. Dusky days and sudden gales were a warning that the sun would soon be gone. Already ice was coming from the Arctic Ocean to seal in the tent city. Soon no ship would be able to get in or out until the following summer. The supply ship must be unloaded and sail at once, or risk freezing into the ice. A lighter, or small barge, was rigged up to unload the goods.

Then, as the loaded lighter swung beside the ship, all ready to be sent ashore, a gale sprang up. The wind came suddenly, and tossed the waves high. There was a roar and a crash, and the loaded lighter barge smashed free, tossing its cargo into the fury of the waves. The anxious watchers on shore saw lumber and boxes filled with medicines, food and clothing tossed into the sea. Men waded out and pulled in some of it, but most of the cargo was lost.

The ship itself had to beat its way offshore and head out to sea as quickly as it could. Nome, city of tents, gold and sand, was isolated until the next summer. The miners pitched in and salvaged every piece of lumber they could. Working together, they built Dr. Wirt's hospital.

There were a few women in the camp, and they came to help Mrs. Wirt and the doctors and nurses take care of the sick. Before long it became too cold to dig on the beach, even with fires going in an attempt to thaw the sand. The camp settled into a quiet broken only by the howling of dogs and the noise from the gambling tents.

From the Eskimos Dr. Wirt bought a fine team of huskies. The leader was a big dog named Whiskers. The doctor, running behind his dogs, went out over the snow with his basket-shaped sled and brought his patients in to the hospital. This was the ambulance in Nome. He called the hospital by the name of one in Switzerland, the Hospice of St. Bernard. And he trained husky and malamute dogs of the North to go out and find lost men in the snows, as the St. Bernard dogs were trained to do in the Alps.

Miners who were "sitting out the winter" spent their time reading anything that they could get to read. Or they carved ivory, learning from the Eskimos how to shape delicate figures out of walrus tusks. They cut and sewed their own mukluks and mittens of sealskin. Or they played cards until the greasy decks wore out completely.

Toward spring the camp faced real hunger. Food stocks were counted and rationed. With care they would last until open water came again, but no longer. The camp would be all right—*if* the first ship in carried food.

Although no white man had ever crossed Alaska in mid-winter before, Dr. Wirt decided that someone must make the trip cross-country to be sure of food by summer. He got his team of seven strong huskies ready. Mrs. Wirt gave him a pillowcase filled with cooked baked beans, frozen hard. When mealtime came around the

doctor could chop off a corner and fry it.

With his huskies, led by Whiskers, he started out with an Eskimo guide, who would leave him at the first Eskimo village. There he would get a new guide who would go with him to the next village. Above his head the northern lights swayed and lit the sky with strange moving shapes in reds, yellows, blues and greens. They crackled with electricity. Hour after hour the dogs ran tirelessly over the snows. The doctor kept his face covered, to prevent freezing, and with his gloved hands gripped the gee-pole of the sled. The end of his journey lay a thousand miles to the south.

Back in Nome nobody really believed that Dr. Wirt would make it. Then, months later, as the sea melted and began to wash against the gray sands of the beach, there was a shout. A ship was on the horizon, and on it was Dr. Wirt with food. He had been all the way to Washington and had gotten aid for Nome. There were plans for schools and churches and a better hospital. Also, a shipment of lumber was on the way.

All over Alaska people were talking of the gold strike at Nome. The beach became a first line of claims. Then farther back there was a second line of diggings. Beyond that there was a third. More and more miners came in, until the town was another Skagway. It was another roaring, noisy place packed and jammed with men sure that no matter how many times they had been disappointed before, here they would at last be lucky.

20

Glittering sands

Among the many stampeders heading for the Klondike was a man named Rex Beach. He came from Tampa, Florida, by way of Chicago. The day that he read about the gold in Alaska and the Klondike he quit his job, and bought a leather suit and a rifle to take up north. He also carried his mandolin. He took the "easy" way up from the mouth of the Yukon, and was frozen in at Rampart City, about halfway to Dawson. Hearing of gold on Minook Creek, Beach joined other miners and went there. He found a cabin, and moved in with a partner.

Rex Beach went prospecting by day, and came back to the cabin to spend a good many of his evenings quarreling with his partner. This man had taken an Indian wife called Short and Dirty, and Beach didn't like her. The two partners almost came to blows wherever they met, even on the street in Rampart. One day the miners called a meeting to settle the dispute between Beach and his partner.

"Boys, let 'em fight it out," suggested one man. The others agreed.

Rex and his partner sailed into each other with a couple of fierce blows. Then suddenly they stopped. What was the quarrel? They couldn't remember. So they shook hands and went back to their cabin to share a supper cooked by Short and Dirty.

When Rex Beach left Chicago he had thought that his rifle would be his most valuable possession. As things turned out, it was his mandolin that proved to be most important. He had no luck with prospecting, but he found that he could make a few dollars playing and singing for the miners. He played for squaw dances, when silent miners and Indian women jogged solemnly about on the rough-hewn log floor. He played "Turkey in the Straw" and other songs, including:

> Buffalo gals won't you come out tonight,
> Come out tonight.
> Buffalo gals won't you come out tonight,
> And dance by the light of the moon.

"Only," a sourdough said, "there ain't no moon. And no dancing as could rightly be called by the name of dancing. Not in polite society, that is."

By day, when he could get a job, Rex Beach worked a hand windlass. As a paid laborer he received five dollars a day and beans. He learned a lot and, like Jack London, stored up the tales that he heard. One of his books, written years later, was based on these stories. It was called *The Barrier*.

During his second winter in the North, Rex Beach went to Dawson, and then returned to Rampart. He still played and sang for the miners, who danced together when there were no squaws. The men substituting for girls had rags tied around their arms.

In the summer of 1899 Rex Beach joined the new stampede down the Yukon River to the port of St. Michaels, and then up to the beaches of Nome. The magic word now was Nome. Everybody talked about Nome.

"Say, you heard about Nome?" they would ask. "Gold is in the sands, just lying there to be picked up. Maybe have to sift it out a little, but that's all."

When Beach jumped out of the small landing boat and waded ashore he found the place already crowded with miners. It had grown till its population numbered three thousand. And there were no Mounties here to keep order. As he walked through town he saw many men that he knew or recognized by sight. They were here from Dawson, from Circle, from Rampart, and from the diggings on the Klondike. Prospectors were fanning out into outlying areas, gulches and creeks, staking claims.

The town grew rapidly and by 1900 Nome was the largest settlement in Alaska Territory. It had more than twelve thousand people. On the streets one might have thought himself in the Dawson of two years before. Rubbing shoulders were men from everywhere. There were some women—dance-hall girls, housewives, and school-teachers. And there were even a few children. The usual sound of howling huskies filled the air. Eskimos came in from their villages with teams of dogs and with babies nodding on the backs of the women.

"There's Tex Rickard," somebody pointed out. "You remember him in Dawson?"

On his arrival in Nome Rickard was penniless, and yet within a year he had a hundred thousand dollars. He was still promoting prize fights.

"Who's that man?" a bystander asked. "I think I used to see him in Dawson, too." The man referred to was Raymond Robins, a young lawyer who had been among the first to stampede to the Klondike from San Francisco. Robins had not found pay dirt in the Yukon Territory. He was in Nome doing some mining and also helping the ill and destitute. When he returned to the States he went to Chicago to devote himself to social service. Later he became an authority on Russia, and an advisor to the President of the United States.

Nome had banks, hotels, stores, and weekly mail service. The mail was brought by dog teams in winter. Here, where ice floes piled up thirty feet high on the beach in winter, miners were digging gold—and gambling it away as they had done in Dawson.

Besides the gamblers, there were outlaws, and for a while holdups were frequent in Nome.

The town soon seemed like the old West.

Rex Beach didn't strike it lucky here, either. So he got out his mandolin again and became an entertainer. Dressed in a loud checked suit, with his face blacked like a minstrel showman, he danced, played and sang. He also told jokes, and amused the miners by eating the buttons from his coat. (They were oyster crackers carefully tied on.) Then he had an idea for making money. He went back to Chicago and interested some wealthy men in sending dredging machinery to Nome.

As he watched the machinery being unloaded from ship to lighter, one of the furious gales of the North came on. It tossed the little boat about like a chip on mountainous waves, and sent the machinery plunging into the sea. Rex Beach, once more without luck, got out his mandolin again.

When he left Nome, Beach was only twenty-four years old. He had not gathered in a fortune in gold. But he had found a wife there—a young girl who ran a boarding house. Also, he had found material for a novel and was ready to begin a writing career. He called his novel *The Spoilers*. It told of the struggle waged between honest prospectors and crooked claim jumpers for the rich sands of Nome, and it became a best-seller.

By 1903 more than two and a half million dollars' worth of gold had been taken from the sands along the shore, most of it by placer, or hand, mining. When the miners could no longer find paying claims, or when their mines ran out, they were off again to a new strike.

It seemed as if new strikes were being made every few days. "What's that? Gold on Copper River? I'm off tomorrow," one miner would say.

"Gold? Fifty cents to the pan? You don't say. Where is Fairbanks? How do you get there?" another wanted to know.

There were strikes in many other places—with miners rushing, pushing, by boat, by dog sled, on foot, all trying to get there first!

But none of the new strikes was big. There was never another Klondike. Or another Nome. The wild stampede to the North was really over. There would never be another like it.

Sourdoughs

Cabins were abandoned and camps became ghost towns. Moss grew on the logs and in summer sagging sod roofs became gardens of wild flowers. In the streets of Dawson grass grew in the ruts made by wagon wheels and sled runners. Across the river Lousetown fell apart and disappeared altogether. A few hundred people still lived in Dawson. One of them was a young clerk named Robert W. Service.

In the dark days of winter Service wrote verses about gold rush days—about the Rag-time Kid, a lady named Lou, Sam McGee and Dangerous Dan McGrew. Somehow these verses captured the spell of the Yukon and the call of the wilderness. They brought back to the men who had been in the big stampede the feeling of those roaring towns. They made them think of lonely cabins, and of creeks and gulches and hills. Somehow the verses seemed to have in them the sudden luck of the rich claim, and the sadness of the trail. They had in them the excitement and the gamble of the sourdough's life.

But now things were different on the creeks and their "pups." Smoke no longer hung low over the thousands of fires set to thaw earth and gold. Now, in the cold air, cabins and tents were falling down. Picks, pans and shovels lay about, rusting along with mountains of empty tin cans. Big dredges and hydraulic hoses took out the gold. It became a regular business. The whole territory of Alaska settled down to regular business, too.

In the Pioneer's Home in Sitka old sourdoughs now talk of those days when they were young. They tell of days when they climbed mountains in deep snow, lived on beans, moosemeat and

sourdough bread. They relive the days when they ran along frozen rivers behind teams of tough and valiant malamutes. They talk about gold, and the lucky ones who found a lot of it.

"Remember Big Alex McDonald?" one will say. "Sure enough, who could forget him? Know what happened to him? He owned near about as many claims as there were in half of Yukon Territory. King of the Klondike, he was! Lost most of it one way or another. They say he ended up living all alone in a cabin on Clearwater Creek."

"I recall Swiftwater Bill in Dawson," another will break in. "That little fellow they called the Knight of the Golden Omelet. He kept right on marrying girl after girl, and running like sixty from his mothers-in-law. Every time he got caught up with he was arrested for bigamy. Every time he lost his money, he went right out and made another rich strike and came in with another fortune. They do say in the end he got away to South America and went to silver mining. Don't know for sure, though. That's just what they say."

There were others who didn't make their pile of gold in the Klondike or Nome stampedes. They made it in business after they went home. Yet there was a gleam in their eyes when they talked of those gold rush days. One of these was Augustus Mack, from New York, who returned home to start a factory making Mack trucks.

"And whatever happened to that gunman from the States, Buckskin Leslie?" old sourdoughs will ask. "Or that gal from Deadwood, Calamity Jane? Or Flora Shaw, the lady reporter from London who climbed White Pass in long skirts looking like a princess? What did happen to them? They just seemed to fade out."

But everybody knew what happened to Belinda Mulroney, the most famous woman stampeder. She married a foreigner, the Count de Carbonneau.

Some said he wasn't really a count, but only a barber from Montreal, Canada. But he found his fortune, and so did Belinda. They went to Paris and lived like royalty before returning to the West and settling there.

"Ever read those stories by Rex Beach? Or Jack London?" an old-timer may ask. "That dog in Jack London's book, *The Call of the Wild*, was really Belinda's dog Buck, you know. The Klondike and Nome made a lot of writers famous."

And what of Carmack and his two Indian friends? Americans gave Carmack the credit for the first discovery of gold on the Bonanza. But Canadians claim that Henderson found it first on Gold Bottom Creek, and told Carmack. Carmack took Kate, his Indian wife, to the United States, but she couldn't fit in there. He sent her back home to Yukon Territory, where she died a few years later. Siwash George married again and lived with his wife in Seattle, enjoying his fortune.

Skookum Jim and Tagish Charley found treasure and left their Indian villages. Charley bought a small hotel. But Skookum Jim, even though he was a millionaire, left it all to wander about with pan and pick, like any old sourdough. He was still looking for luck in the creeks and gulches. Henderson? Why, he never found much. The Canadian government finally gave him a life pension.

The stampede surged over Dyea, the Scales, Sheep Camp and Chilkoot Pass, and left nothing behind. The town disappeared. The stopping places on the long, bitter climb were deserted and the trail itself blotted out by the snows and the winds.

The majestic Yukon River, once crowded with thousands of steamboats, rafts, canoes and barges, is quiet again. Modern traffic moves north on highways across streams, swamps and mountains. Over White Pass, where men went crazy and horses died by the thousands, there is a railroad. Skagway, Nome, Fairbanks, Juneau, Sitka—all are attractive towns or cities now, and Dawson is a small town full of memories of the great gold rush days. Airplanes carry people over the still lonely land of roaming moose, caribou, bears and wolves. Bush pilots fly from lake to lake, from river to town, in the time a good dog team would take to travel only a few miles.

The reindeer herd that arrived too late to help

Dawson was the beginning of the domesticated herds that are now valuable to the Eskimos. With others brought in later they have become a good source of meat, leather, and transportation.

In Alaska, where Mount McKinley—the highest mountain on the North American continent—raises its white peak to the sky, men still wander about with pick and pan. And they go up and down the creeks and mountains of the Canadian Yukon. A few still hang their cans of sourdough above the stoves. A few still wash and sift gravel for the few bits of gold at the bottom of a pan.

But of the two hundred thousand people who started the long trails to the Klondike gold country, not more than thirty thousand reached Dawson. Not more than three or four thousand found any gold. Of those who did strike it rich, only a few managed to keep their fortunes. It was the same story in Nome. Most of those who really profited from the gold rush were those who sold things and those who, in one way or another, took the gold away from the miners.

Yet there was not a man or woman who got there and returned who did not come to look back on the experience as the big moment of his or her life. The big excitement! The big adventure! They fought their way through. They refused to give up. Most of them were young men, and they were glad that they went.

The gold rush helped pull the United States out of its financial panic. More money was spent to buy equipment and supplies than was taken out of the earth in the North. With the gold that was mined and the money that went into circulation the United States and Canada became more prosperous.

Up there on the creeks and rivers where the gold came from there are still many tall tales that are told. The Indians have their own stories. Stampeders whirling down the Yukon sometimes crashed to their death against two rocks standing out of the foaming water. These the Indians call the Old Woman and the Old Man. They say that the squaw nagged and screamed at her husband until he flung her into the river, where she turned into a rock. And the brave, standing waist deep in the stream, was also turned to stone. Only the cheechacos who knew enough to let the current take them along could safely pass the Old Woman and the Old Man.

Miners can tell you of the sourdough who grew the longest and thickest set of whiskers in all the North country. All winter they grew as he dug and shoveled, and all summer too he let them grow as he washed out the gold from the dirt. When he finally arrived in Dawson to spend his gold, he had his whiskers cut off. The barber panned out the whiskers, and came up with a hundred dollars' worth of gold dust!

A listener may ask:

"Was that the same miner who made such good sourdough bread that it rose and rose in the oven till it raised the stove itself up to the roof and then took it right on through?"

"No, that was his partner," the miner telling the story will answer. "And he never did get his stove back. The last time he got a glimpse of it, the pesky thing was sailing for the North Pole."

"And what about that stampeder who froze solid while he was leaning over to light his stove?"

The miner has the answer to that question, too.

"If you spend a winter in this land at the ends of the earth, perhaps you will see the ghost of Sam the Sourdough as he passes by you like a white mist on the snowy trail. On his bearded face there is a grin of hope. There is a pack on his back, and in his hands an empty coffee can, ready for the gold dust and nuggets he is sure to find."

Maybe it is the spirit of the Windy Kid, with his dog team? Or of Skookum Jim? Or of the Lucky Swede? Or even of Big Alex, the King of the Klondike? Maybe he is the ghost of every old sourdough of the old days—of the last great Gold Rush—who pushed on to the end of the last frontier.

index

72, 75–77, 155, 156, 170, 178
Long-Toms, 19
Long Trail, *see* Ashcroft Trail
Lousetown, *see* Klondike City
Lynn Canal, 42, 86

Mack, August, 177
Mackenzie River, 9, 88, 94, 137
Malamute Kid, 156
May West (boat), 81, 100
McDonald, Alex, 105–106, 123, 177, 182
McEwen, George A., 127–128
McPhee, Bill, 153
McQuesten, LeRoy Napoleon, 15, 21, 27–28, 31, 33
Miles Canyon, 75
Miller, Joaquin, 101, 110–111
Millet, O. B., 118
Minook (Indian), 83
Minook Creek, 83
Mint, U. S., 37
Mizner, Addison, 21, 111
Mizner, Edgar, 21–22, 111
Mizner, Wilson, 21, 111, 112
Moodie, Inspector, 94
Moore, Captain, 42–43, 44–45, 48, 49
Moosehide (Indian village), 28, 86, 135
Moosehide Creek, 99
Mount McKinley, 2, 180
Mounted Police, *see* Canadian Mounted Police
Mueller, Mr., 61–62
Mukluk, The (boat), 81
Mulroney, Belinda, 107–109, 111, 132, 152, 153, 178

New Racket (steamboat), 28
Nome, Alaska, 159–167, 170–173, 179, 180
Nugget, The (newspaper), 96, 112

Oatley Sisters, 112
Ottawa, Canada, 63, 64, 85, 126

"Panning," 18
Pantages, Alexander, 111
Peace River, 88, 92
Peace River Trail, 87
Peel River, 94
Peterson, Mr., 117
"Placer" mining, 18, 173
Pleasant Camp, 56
Porcupine Creek, 29, 30, 137
Portland (ship), 34, 37–38, 96
Preacher's Creek, 29
Pyramid Harbor, Alaska, 86

Rabbit Creek, 13, 15, 16, 17, 122
Rampart City, 83, 169, 170
Reid, Frank, 48, 145–150
Rickard, Tex, 112, 171
Robins, Raymond, 171
Russians, 5, 8

St. Michael (boat), 83, 84
St. Michaels, Alaska, 8, 36, 37, 82, 83, 156, 159, 170
Salvation Army, 125
Sam "the moose," 151, 152, 155
San Francisco, California, 34–37, 38, 54, 79, 96, 156, 171
San Francisco *Call*, 36
Scales, 57, 61, 179